T0192976

BOOK MARKETING FOR AUTHORS

Get Ready, Get Set, Succeed!

TERRI ANN LEIDICH AND JULIE BROMLEY

North Carolina

Book Marketing for Authors: Get Ready, Get Set, Succeed!
© 2021 Terri Ann Leidich and Julie Bromley. All rights reserved.

No part of this book may be reproduced or transmitted in any form or by any means, electronic or mechanical, including photocopying, recording, or by any information storage and retrieval system, without permission in writing from the publisher.

The information and recommendations in this book are presented in good faith and for informational purposes only. Every effort has been made to ensure the materials presented are accurate and current. All information is supplied on the condition that the reader or any other person receiving this information will perform their own due diligence and make their own determination as to its suitability for any purpose prior to use of this information. The purpose of this material is to educate. The authors and publisher shall have neither liability nor responsibility to any person or entity with respect to loss or damage caused, or alleged to have been caused, directly or indirectly, by the information contained in this book.

The external links are being provided as a convenience and for informational purposes only; they do not constitute an endorsement or an approval by WriteLife Publishing and the authors of any of the products, services or opinions of the corporation or organization or individual. WriteLife Publishing bears no responsibility for the accuracy, legality, or content of the external site or for that of subsequent links. Contact the external site for answers to questions regarding its content.

Published in the United States by WriteLife Publishing
(an imprint of Boutique of Quality Books Publishing Company, Inc.)
www.writelife.com

Printed in the United States of America

978-1-60808-245-2 (p)
978-1-60808-246-9 (e)

Library of Congress Control Number: 2021937129

Book design by Robin Krauss, www.bookformatters.com
Cover design by Rebecca Lown, www.rebeccalowndesign.com
Editor: Allison Itterly

Praise for
Book Marketing for Authors
and for
Terri Ann Leidich and Julie Bromley

"*Book Marketing for Authors* contains a wealth of valuable information. This guide for both traditionally published and self-published authors, is a book to be read, reread, and kept close for reference. Within the pages, every aspect of book marketing receives a thorough discussion in easy-to-understand steps and assessable language. Why try to reinvent the wheel? I'm happy to let the combined wisdom of professionals in the field save me the time. This book has inspired me to see marketing in a new way. And as the authors continually say, keeping it fun."

— Margaret Lukas,
author of *River People* and *The Broken Statue*

"*Book Marketing for Authors* is absolutely dedicated to your success as an author. Every facet of publishing and the business of being an author is detailed in this book. It is a balance of bullet points and clear descriptions that immediately amplify the route to take to make your book known to the world. Terri Leidich and Julie Bromley know what they are doing. They have guided my success and my five books continue to sell in over 40 countries."

— Tina Zion,
author of *Be Your Own Medical Intuitive*

"*Book Marketing for Authors* by Terri Ann Leidich and Julie Bromley is a clear-eyed manual that will help any author, whether they are self-published, with an indy press, or even a major publishing house, to market their books more successfully.

Leidich and Bromley have years of experience helping authors succeed in the marketplace. They have distilled that experience into a blueprint that is concise, but comprehensive. They cover everything from defining your brand to building a website to establishing a social media presence to creating and implementing a marketing plan.

The book is packed with information. What makes it an exceptional resource, is that Leidich and Bromley understand, having published several hundred books, that every writer is unique and what works for some will not work for others. They make it clear that there isn't one magical path to success. They encourage authors to develop a plan they are comfortable with.

Book marketing is a business and if you want your book to find a readership, you have to come up with an effective marketing program. *Book Marketing for Authors* is an excellent resource for helping an author achieve that goal."

— Len Joy,
author of *Everyone Dies Famous*

"*Book Marketing for Authors, Get Ready, Get Set, Succeed!* by Terri Ann Leidich and Julie Bromley explains everything a new author needs to know, presented in a logical, organized, and straightforward format. The book is not so long as to get bogged down in its reading. Instead, it takes each major subject, explains its importance and how to approach it, then directs you to websites or organizations where you can learn in more detail, if desired. It stresses that you do not have to do everything, but rather, focus on things that come naturally to you. Most importantly, it gives you a timeline of what you should do when. For example, endorsements and editorial reviews should be sought at least three or four months prior to the book's release. This enables the publisher to incorporate good reviews on the back cover or within the book on the "praise page."

I cannot say enough about *Book Marketing for Authors*. Its clarity and its excellent advice ranks it high above other "how to" books on this subject. I know because I have looked!"

— Patricia M. Meier,
Media Manager for Daniel V. Meier, Jr, author of *The Dung Beetles of Liberia; No Birds Sing Here;* and *Bloodroot.*

"There are many books on the craft of writing but few on the essential task of marketing a book. Leidich and Bromley offer a comprehensive look at all aspects of marketing needed to become a successful author."

— Fauzia Burke,
author of *Online Marketing for busy Authors,*
President of FSB Associates, and Co-Founder of Pub Site

TABLE OF CONTENTS

GET SET

SUCCEED

ABOUT THIS BOOK

Y ou've finished writing your book, so now what? Many writers think their work is done at that point. But once a book is published, writers become authors and marketing becomes a big part of their job.

As a publisher, a writer, and an author, I want things to be simple and straightforward when it comes to book marketing. When I finished my first book and began the task of marketing it, I was a bit overwhelmed. From my perspective, most marketing books can be too convoluted and wordy. Keep it simple! As an author, I want to know the essentials of what I need to do to market my book, and when I need to do them. From there, I'll figure out if it's something that I can do and will enjoy doing, or if I need to hire some help. And that's the way we approached this book.

This book is divided into three sections:

- **Get Ready** (the essentials that need to be done before your book is released)
  - If you've already published your book and haven't done the essential work, then do it now.
- **Get Set** (establishing an ongoing marketing plan)
- **Succeed** (the essentials that need to continually be done to keep your book getting attention and selling)

We've kept the sections straightforward with explanations and lists that you can check off as you go.

Don't get overwhelmed. Take it one step at a time. You'll learn that marketing is never wasted, but it also typically doesn't show immediate results. It is a marathon, not a sprint. So believe in yourself and your book and put processes in place.

And most of all, enjoy the journey!

GET READY

INTRODUCTION

Marketing Is Your Responsibility

Writers are often under the misconception that once their book is published—whether self-published or by a publisher (either hybrid or traditional)—their work is done and they can move on to writing the next book. In actuality, that is when the work really begins.

Marketing is your responsibility. Going from an unknown author to a well-known author or a bestselling author takes work. Writing a book is just the first step toward success; the rest is continuous marketing from you and your team (e.g., publisher, publicist, street team, marketing person). If you don't do the continuous work, you won't get the sales or well-known author status. It's that simple. Even if you have a team working with you, it is still imperative that you be involved in building relationships with readers, bookstores, libraries, etc.

For many authors, the word *marketing* sends them into a panic. "I'm not good at selling," they'll say. Well good. Because marketing is not *selling*. Marketing is about building a brand and relationships so people will know who you are and what you write. That's how you build a following and a fan base, which creates sales for your books.

If you have a publisher, their main job is to help ensure you are bringing a strong, quality product to the marketplace and that you have distribution and discoverability. If you self-publish, all of the above, including marketing, falls on your shoulders.

Every publisher, whether large or small, has marketing tools for each book they publish. But every author is still responsible for a large part of marketing their book. Author involvement in today's publishing environment is crucial for success. No one can build your brand but you, so you must take charge of your own marketing. There are major elements that need to be strongly considered as part of your marketing plan, all of which will be discussed in this book.

We all have different personalities and approaches to life. You can use your strengths to build an effective marketing plan. If you're shy, you may flourish on social media. If you like public speaking, you may shine at a book reading. In today's world, there are a myriad of choices, but if you want to be successful, you have to market your book.

Approach this book and the ideas in it with a "think outside the box" mentality to help you stand out in a positive, creative way. The most important part is to not get so caught up with expectations that you don't enjoy the process! Publishing a book is one of the most exciting things anyone can do, so take a deep breath and get ready to succeed!

CHAPTER 1

TREATING YOUR BOOK AS A BUSINESS

Many writers don't realize that when you publish a book—either through a publisher or self-publishing—you are stepping into the business of publishing. And it is a business.

Movies and headlines make the publishing process sound simple: You write a book, you get it published, and then you sit back and collect the royalty checks. This couldn't be further from the truth. As an author, you are becoming a business owner with a product to sell. And as a business owner, you are responsible for creating that product, and, in some form, getting it out into the marketplace.

Approaching Your Book as a Business

Your book is finally ready for public consumption. Your book is no longer a spark of an idea that started years ago while you were sitting in traffic or lying awake at night when you couldn't sleep. Your book is now a product.

There are many benefits of approaching your book as a business. Not only are you getting your book out into the world, but you are also creating a name for yourself as an author. This type of exposure can create a host of other opportunities (i.e., having a big following on social media).

Another benefit of treating your book like a business is the monetary gain. You can earn royalties—maybe not right away, but if you continue to invest time and money, results will come.

New York Times best-selling books get to that list because they are strongly marketed.

If your book is successful, your publisher may be willing to publish your other books and work with you long-term. But if you don't put time and continued effort into your book, you risk being dropped by your publisher if having your book in the marketplace costs them more money than it makes in sales.

A business will not be successful if there isn't a strong foundation in place. Businesses have expectations attached to them, such as expenses and tax responsibilities. Taking on the business of marketing your book is no different. Chances are this is unfamiliar territory, so you'll be starting from the ground up. It's time to start thinking of your book as a product. Our goal is to help you figure out what methods will work best and play to your strengths so you can succeed.

You Must Invest to Create Success

Businesses take a committed investment and can generally create a return on your investment if your investment is planned and consistent. Selling your book will require an investment of two things:

- Your time
- Your money

You've written your book, but now you have to dedicate your time to make that book successful. Here are few things that you'll need to do:

- Create a marketing plan
- Dedicate a marketing budget
- Make marketing a part of your weekly activities

• Constantly be open to learning and participating in marketing opportunities

If you're serious about marketing your book, you should know that there is a cost. How you create your budget is up to you, but money will be spent on things such as:

• Marketing opportunities

• Creating marketing collateral

• Education or training about book marketing

When Does Marketing Begin?

At least six months or more before the release of your book, you should begin marketing your book and building your author brand. If you wait until the month before your release, you've missed opportunities for:

• Building platforms on social media (Facebook, Instagram, Goodreads, Twitter, etc.)

• Gaining or adding to your fan base

• Creating or updating your website

• Collecting emails for a newsletter

• A cover reveal

• Pre-release endorsements

• Building buzz by releasing snippets of your book

• Building a street team

• Offering opportunities for ARCs (Advance Release Copies)

All of these bullet points will be discussed at length in the chapters that follow to help you understand the many facets of marketing and how to make them work for you and your book.

CHAPTER 2

BUILDING YOUR AUTHOR BRAND

B etween one and three million eBooks, audiobooks, and books in print are released into the marketplace each year. That's a lot of competition!

Why do some mediocre books make it to the bestselling lists while great books sometimes languish with few sales? The difference is how well an author brand is developed and the size of an author's fan base. Remember, books on the *New York Times* bestseller list are not necessarily the best books written, but they have been well marketed. The cornerstone of book marketing is building your author brand so readers will know who you are and will want to follow you. Readers don't generally follow publishers; they follow authors. It is you and your writing they are interested in.

What Is an Author Brand?

Your author brand is your promise to your readers. It is the entire package of how you present yourself and your book to the world. Your social media persona, website design, and your book genre are just a few ways to communicate how you want readers to think about you as a writer and as a person. A strong author brand will also help differentiate you from your competitors.

When you hear J.K. Rowling's name, you probably think about Harry Potter. But did you know that she also writes crime fiction under the pen name Robert Galbraith? Rowling has a specific author brand with the Harry Potter franchise that is separate from the books she writes for adults.

A strong author brand is a "message of experience" that tells readers what they can expect from you and why they should care about your books. Effective author branding will help build your writer platform and audience, which in turn will help you market your book.

Designing Your Author Brand

Your author brand is based on:

- Who you are
- Who your ideal reader is
- Your personality
- Your beliefs
- The author image you want to portray
- Your *why* for writing

Before creating your author brand, it's important to become clear on what you want to communicate to readers. Keep in mind that the author image you want to portray may be different from who you are in your personal life, but that is perfectly fine.

Important Parts of Your Author Brand

Every author brand consists of a few key elements:

- A persona
- Author's bio
- Photo
- Logo
- Tagline
- Website

- Media kit
- Social media profiles
- Business cards
- Bookmarks
- A social presence

Creating Your Author Brand

Every author must have an author brand, but sometimes this may not be so clear-cut. If you are a horror writer, your audience won't expect you to write a steamy romance novel. Sometimes it can be difficult to discover or categorize what you want your author brand to be.

Here are a few things to think about when building your author brand:

- How do you want to be known? What persona do you want to portray? Will you use a pen name?

- Simplify what truly represents you and your writing: your values, interests, passions, and purpose.

- What words, ideas, concepts, and feelings do you want people to associate with you?

- Who is your ideal reader and why?

- How is your work unique from other authors in your genre? How are they branding themselves?

- Check out the websites of authors, bloggers, and other creatives. What attracts you? Notice what they are doing effectively and try adapting some of those concepts to your own brand.

Building your brand can be a challenge because you have to step away and look at yourself and how you want the world to see you as an author. Keep in mind that once you have an author brand, it should be consistent across all platforms (social media, your website, the tone of your posts, etc.).

Use your three words

If you are struggling to pinpoint your author brand, choose three words that define you as a writer. For example: *edgy, witty, mysterious,* or *romantic, passionate, daring.* These words can help define who you are as an author and help identify your target audience.

Once you have chosen three words, make sure the essence of those adjectives are coming through as you create your brand. If your writing is *funny, adventurous,* and *caring,* you'll need to ensure that your author brand reflects that. Your persona on social media should be quirky and lighthearted. If you write horror novels, the colors on your website and your book covers should be dark and edgy, not pastel with flowers in the background.

Your why for writing

Creating your author brand should focus on your *why* for writing. If your *why* for writing is to make people laugh, your sense of humor and wit may need to be exaggerated as you build your author brand. If your writing intention is to write about serious issues, then that side of your personality will be a strong part of your author brand.

Author Brand Tips

Here are a few tips to keep in mind when building your author brand:

- A well-written, edited, and formatted book is your best marketing and brand-building tool.
- The key is to brand you, not your book(s).

- Your website must convey who you are in addition to who you are as an author. For example, writing an op-ed column for a political website that expresses your views on an issue.

- Your social media posts should discuss topics other than your books to strengthen your brand. For example, retweeting the Humane Society's posts once a week on your Twitter page, or posting uplifting stories or memes (pictures with words).

- Marketing decisions should be made strategically, always keeping your brand in mind.

- Hard work is necessary to figure out why you write, what your promise is to readers, what differentiates your work, and how to articulate it.

Here are other tools you can use to build your brand, all of which will be discussed in detail in other parts of this book:

- Awards
- Publicity
- Book clubs
- Book reviews and endorsements

To help solidify your understanding of author branding, think about your favorite bestselling authors. Check out the components of their marketing—website, social media, author profile, etc.—and identify what pops out. How are they getting across the message of who they are and what they write? Use that understanding to build your own brand.

When building your author brand, you may continue to tweak your brand for a while, and that's okay. Sometimes when we move from being a writer to an author, it takes a while to really define who we are as an author and what we want to portray to the world. Brand building is a process, so go easy on yourself and enjoy the journey.

CHAPTER 3

GROWING YOUR AUDIENCE

W hat is a musician performing to an empty crowd? What is a sports team playing in an empty arena? What is an author without any readers? An artist needs an audience if he or she wants to make a profit off their art. To be a successful author, you'll need to attract readers, a fan base, and eventually loyal fans who will want to help spread the word about you and your book.

The list below describes some of the activities or programs that you will need to begin building your audience.

- Author website (you gotta have one!)

- Grow a mailing list (e.g., newsletter)

- Create a newsletter

- Write a blog

- Design eye-catching graphics for social media

- Be active on social media

- Participate in book selling and promoting events

- Appear on podcasts

- Recommend other authors' books

- Cross-promote with other authors

Author Website

Every author needs a website! Think of it as the landing spot for all things related to you and your book. Whenever you do any marketing, your website URL should be included.

- Your website is a place for readers to learn about you.
- Your website gives you a platform to grow your brand and fan base.
- Your website can showcase your book, share excerpts from your book, share reviews of your book, and provide links where your books can be purchased.
- Your website URL will show up on internet searches.

Because an author's website is such an important piece of the marketing puzzle, we discuss this at length in chapter 4, "Creating a Website."

Mailing Lists

Having a mailing list is the key to connecting to people who want to know about you and your book. Remember, people wouldn't sign up for your mailing list if they weren't interested. A few things you can do with a mailing list are:

- Email a newsletter or blog
- Send information on an upcoming release
- Notify fans about special events

You can grow your mailing list through your newsletter, your website, and on your social media accounts.

Newsletter

An author newsletter that is sent out on a regular basis can help you stay connected and relevant to your readers as well as help you to continually build your fan base.

Benefits of an author newsletter

- It connects you to readers.
- It helps you build "super fans."
- It continually reminds readers about you and your books.
- Your newsletter stays in the subscriber's inbox until they take action.
- You can continually market or soft sell to readers who have already expressed interest in your books.
- You can do group promotions with other authors through your newsletter.
- You can quickly get reviews and sales on a new release.
- You can promote the print, eBook, and audiobook versions of your book.
- You can ask for feedback on a book title, book cover, etc.
- You can reuse content from your blog posts in smaller bits.
- You can quickly turn social media followers into subscribers by offering them something in return.

Newsletter content

Newsletter content can include things about your book such as:

- A cover reveal
- A release date of your upcoming book
- Awards you've recently won
- Events you are planning
- Any price campaigns (sales) that you or your publisher run on your book or eBook

Creating a newsletter

The first step to creating a newsletter is to pick an email provider. To find an email newsletter software that works best for your needs and budget, do an internet search for "email newsletter software."

The two most popular email providers are:

- Constant Contact (there is a cost for this service)
- MailChimp (there is no cost until you get over 2,000 people on your list)

After you have chosen an email provider:

- Embed a sign-up link into your newsletter so people can share your newsletter, which will give others the option to use the link to sign up.

- Link the newsletter to each page of your website, below your signature on your email, and post it on social media.

- Send your newsletter out on a consistent basis. We recommend sending a newsletter out monthly.

Please note that the email providers listed above require that you have gotten permission from the people you list on your database. This prevents users from buying lists of emails and spamming them with content. This is not an approach you would want to take anyway when you are trying to build a fan base.

How to acquire email addresses for your newsletter

- Use a sign-up link on your website, your social media, and under your email signature.
- Use a sign-up sheet at book signings or events.
- Provide a sign-up link for your website on your bookmark.

- Repost your newsletter info when it appears on your social media.

- Communicate with your fan base that you have a newsletter and suggest they follow it.

Blog

Having a blog is important because you can blog about your work or things connected to you. It's a great way for your fans to see your writing in another form, and it can help build your persona. Remember, blogs should not focus entirely on your books and your writing. They should help to expand a reader's knowledge about you.

- A good blog post is around 1,500–2,000 words. However, shorter blogs of 500–750 words can also work if you are blogging often.

- You can repurpose parts of your blog post as other social media.

- Blogs should be about topics that are of interest to you and your readers.

- Connect your blog to your Amazon Author page.

- You can offer to write a guest post for other people's blogs.

- You can interact with other authors who write or blog in your genre.

Make sure there is a link on your website so people can sign up for your newsletter and/or blog. There should also be an archived section for old newsletters and/or blogs.

Social Media

If you want to build a fan base and a community, you need to be active on social media. Social media is a place for discovery. It is also a place where your author brand can shine. For example, if humor is a part of your author brand, funny stories or snippets on your social media can attract followers because they enjoy your humor. Occasionally mentioning your book on social media can draw readers to you.

The world revolves around social media, which is a great place for marketing. We talk about social media in more detail in chapter 5, "Building Your Social Media Platform."

Events

In the world of publishing, there are many opportunities for authors to participate in book events. A search on the internet for "book events" will bring up a large number of results. It is advised to be specific when researching events that would be a good fit for you, your book, and your budget. Narrow your search to "book events near me," or "book events in my state." Then you can branch outward.

Tips for book events

- Almost every larger community has a book festival that offers opportunities for writers (even those who are not yet well known) for being on panels, renting booths to exhibit and sell your book, or banding in groups with other authors to read or promote your books.

- There are large national events that focus solely on authors such as BookExpo, which is held in New York City every year. Your publisher and/or book distributor will most likely have a booth at BookExpo, and there may be opportunities for you to individually participate in events like book signings, book display, etc. BookExpo also has opportunities for self-published authors to do book signings and promotions.

- The American Library Association holds both regional and national events each year in different locations throughout the country. Each show differs in the opportunities they offer. Your publisher may offer individual opportunities, or they may choose which books they present at each show.

Events can be a very strong part of your marketing plan. If you have a publisher, find out how they communicate these opportunities to you—through email, a newsletter, etc. A great way to get in front of readers is to get your name and book information out at book events, whether you represent yourself or have a publisher.

Cross-Promoting

Recommending other authors' books will not only to help them, but it will expose you and your book to a wider audience. As we often explain to our authors, we are not in competition with each other. If readers read one book in a lifetime, competition would be a concern, but most people who read are voracious readers and are continually on the search for new books. By working with other authors, you can help advertise each other's work to a growing audience.

There are many ways to grow your audience, and these are just a few examples. As you become comfortable with being an author, growing an audience will become a part of what you do. The important thing to understand is that you don't have to "sell" your book to create an audience. Your brand, the books you write, and the interaction that you have with readers will help you automatically grow your fan base.

CHAPTER 4

CREATING A WEBSITE

To be a successful author, it is imperative that you have an author website. Your website should be the major marketing piece in your marketing plan. Without an author website, your marketing plan would be like a car without wheels—perhaps it's nice to look at, but it won't get you anywhere. An author website gives you the vehicle to let readers learn more about you and to help build your community. The more readers can connect with you, the more likely they are to become fans and buy your books.

Your website can be a simple four- to five-page site that provides information about you and your book. You can create your website with a template, or you can find someone to create a website for you. If you have another business website, you still need an author website unless your book is part of your other business. We recently became familiar with a website builder that focuses on helping authors. Their website is https://pub-site.com

Domain Name

The first thing you'll need to do is buy your domain name. A search on the internet will give you a list of the top domain sites and their ratings. We also suggest that you buy the domain for the name of your book so people can be directed to your website when they search for you online. More than one domain name can be pointed to the same website.

Your domain name should be your name or a variation of your

name. For instance, Terri's domain name is TerriAnnLeidich.com. If your name is already taken, you can add your middle name, or you can create a domain with your name followed by the word *author*. If you don't want to use your name, choose a domain name that is easy to find and/or search for online and something that people will connect with you and/or your book.

Essentials of an Author Website

An author website provides information about you as an author, your book, and how to buy your book. These are the essentials of an author website:

- About the Author page
  - This page should contain your picture, your bio, and a small blurb about why you write.
- About the Book page
  - You can give a full description of your book on your website. This is an expanded version of a *book blurb,* which is usually limited to a certain number of words to fit on the back cover or in a limited space provided on social media or in advertising.
- Contact page
- Events page
- Social media buttons so readers can follow you
- Link to your blog (if you have one)
- Link to your newsletter (if you have one)
- Links to top retailers (Amazon, Barnes & Noble, IndieBound, Apple, Google Play, Kobo, etc.)
- Link to an excerpt of your book

- If your eBooks are sold on Overdrive.com, they provide a link to an excerpt for every book they sell. This link can be an easy way to provide a book excerpt without having to create one.

Make sure to keep your website professional and clean, as well as updated and interesting with fresh content. Check out the websites of your favorite authors or the top-selling authors in your genre. As mentioned, your website should provide links for a variety of retailers where people can purchase your book.

Author Profile

An author profile bio is one of the strongest marketing tools for your author brand and your books. Simply put, an author profile is a blurb that informs readers of who you are, what books you've written, and the highlights of your life that will interest them.

We recommend creating an extensive author profile on your website—up to two pages long—from which you can take excerpts for other sites and purposes. You can share all or parts of your author profile on sites that are influential in getting the word out about you and your book.

You should post your author profile on these four major websites:

- Amazon
- Goodreads
- BookBub
- LinkedIn

Each website may differ in terms of the type of information you can post on your author profile. Get familiar with each site to know what they are looking for. Here are a few things that you may be able to include in your author profile:

- Links to your book
- Your author information basics
- Your author photo (this gives readers an opportunity to visually connect with you)
- Links to your videos
- Photos of book signings, with readers, etc.
- Links to your blog

An author profile on Amazon is strategic! If you don't put your author profile anywhere else, put it there! We discuss more about the benefits of using Amazon in chapter 9, "The Power of Amazon."

CHAPTER 5

BUILDING YOUR SOCIAL MEDIA PLATFORM

I n today's world, social media is how people engage, discover new things, and build online relationships. If you're an author, social media is a big must! Ignoring social media and its impact is paramount to turning your head away from success as an author. While social media doesn't necessarily sell books, it is a strong marketing tool, and is important for building your author brand and a fan base. Readers want to know about the authors they follow!

There are tons of books on the market that can guide you through setting up social media accounts and profiles. There are also free social media tutorials on the internet. Find an option that will work for you. If you don't want to be active on social media, find someone who will manage your account(s) for you. Social media can expand awareness of you and your book across the world with just a few clicks on a keyboard.

While social media can be a powerful tool in connecting us through technology, it's important to be smart in how you use it. Don't give away any highly personal information on any social media account.

Using Social Media

A good rule of thumb for using social media is to focus more on the social aspect and less on marketing. People use social media to socialize, so use your posts for things that may interest your audience and engage them in conversations.

- Share, comment, like posts—use friendly input, not hard sales, to gain attention.

- Social media is a great place to let your personality shine through so followers will become interested in you and then in your writing.

- In today's world, marketing is as much "word of eye" as it is "word of mouth," so use visuals (e.g., photos, memes, graphics).

Social Media Sites

Each social media site has its own approach and following. At the time of this writing, the top social media sites are:

- Facebook
  - It is currently the top site in popularity.
  - You can have an author page as well as a personal profile.
  - You can create a separate group for your street team.
  - You can add an editor to post on your behalf.
  - You can promote and boost posts on Facebook.
- YouTube
  - It is very visual and multifaceted.
  - You can post book trailer videos, author interviews, chats with authors, etc.
  - Post training videos if your book is instructional or in the self-help genre.
- Instagram

- A picture is worth a thousand words, and Instagram is filled with pictures.

- There is no character or caption limit, and the content is fresh and free-flowing.

- You can set up your account so that your posts on Instagram will also post on other social media sites such as Facebook.

• Twitter

- One of the most widely used of the social media apps.

- It's a quick and easy way to ingratiate yourself to readers and potential readers.

- It is intended for simple, short, casual connections.

- Fast and succinct with a limit to the number of characters that can be in any one post.

- Effective tweeting takes creativity. You must be interesting for people to be interested. Twitter is definitely a platform for personalities.

• Tumblr

- A blogging and social media tool that allows users to publish a "tumblelog" or short blog posts.

- Tumblr is not quite as popular as it used to be, but as a site it's still very much alive.

• Reddit

- A social news platform that allows users to discuss and vote on content that other users have submitted.

• LinkedIn

- This site is perfect for nonfiction authors as it allows you to reach executives and professionals.

- LinkedIn groups are a great place to promote content from your blog and to have focused conversations.

• Snapchat

- Lets you easily talk with friends, view Live Stories from around the world, and explore news in the Discover feature.

• Pinterest

- A high percentage of users on Pinterest (98% at this writing) are women, so if women are a large part of your target market, Pinterest is a social media platform that you need to consider.

- Visuals (e.g., photos, graphs, memes with positive sayings) are very popular on Pinterest.

Social Media Scheduling Sites

Being active on social media on a consistent basis is key. Your marketing plan should include weekly posts on all of your social media accounts. These posts should cover a variety of topics, not just your book.

How you engage on social media is up to you. Some authors prefer to engage with social media on a daily basis, choosing different sites for each day. For example, Monday is for Facebook and Twitter, Tuesday is for Instagram, etc. But there are other ways to manage your social media postings. There are sites that schedule posts ahead of time. If you use a scheduling service, you are able to create all your posts for a week or more that you want to appear later on different sites. It's that simple.

At the time of this writing, here are the popular social media scheduling sites:

- Hootsuite (https://hootsuite.com)
- Buffer (https://buffer.com)
- Sprout Social (https://sproutsocial.com)
- TweetDeck (https://tweetdeck.twitter.com)
- SocialOomph (www.socialoomph.com)

Every social media scheduling site is different. Some sites are free, while others have a cost. Some sites will work with only one or two social media channels, so make sure you choose the correct site for your marketing plan. You could use a scheduling site for several of your social media accounts and personally post on a few others. Whatever you decide, these sites provide options for organizing your social media marketing.

Tips and Tricks for Social Media

Whether you are a social media pro or just getting started, we've compiled a few tips and tricks on how to fully benefit from using social media to market your book.

Spread the news

- Make sure your social media usernames are consistent for all social media accounts.
- Include your major social media URLs on your business card.
- Put your social media share buttons on each blog post, newsletter, email signature, etc.
- Link your social media accounts on the Contact and About You pages of your website.

Gather followers

- Use photos (of you, your book, of people reading your book, etc.). Photos get more visibility and attention than text-only posts.

- Be responsive through social media. Let your followers know you know they are following you.

- Post consistently. You may decide to post once a day, every other day, or once a week. The frequency is up to you. Keep it consistent so your followers will get used to seeing your posts.

Engage with and follow others

- Re-share other people's content.
- Be relatable.
- Videos on YouTube have become a strong part of social media and give authors an easy and inexpensive way to reach out to their established audience and attract new fans.

- Follow your publisher and your favorite authors on social media.

- Follow social media accounts of influencers on topics related to your book (e.g., fellow authors or experts in a relevant field).

- Engage with influencers. Share and respond to their posts, which could trigger them to follow you, thus introducing you to their followers.

- Follow people who engage positively with you on social media and respond to their questions and comments.

Keep it interesting

- Give attention to your social media profiles. Make sure they are positive and attractive.

- People shouldn't have to guess that you are an author. Make that statement on every social media account.

- Share interesting content that is either directly or indirectly related to the kind of things you write about.

- Share parts of your life—funny stories, pictures from your travels, favorite things, etc. Remember, readers want to get to know you too. You are the brand!

Don't make excuses

- Don't let concern or fear of receiving negative feedback stop you from participating on social media. Those people can be unfollowed, muted, or blocked, and the posts can be deleted.

Use images

- The internet, social media, and marketing thrive on images.

- Authors need more than pictures of their book to keep social media relevant and interesting.

- If you are unsure of what images to use, follow a couple of your favorite bestselling authors and get a sense of what they post and the types of images that are being used.

- Create memes on sites such as Canva and Adobe to post on your social media accounts.

Promotional Posts

While social media needs to be about much more than promoting your book, here are a few ways to effectively promote your book:

- A short book synopsis
- Book reviews
- Book descriptions (also called *book blurbs*)
- Announcing sales or promotions
- Sharing author event info
- Award announcements

When you post about your book, always include a link to your website or the order links for retail sites where your book can be purchased.

The most important information to take away from this chapter is that you absolutely need social media as a part of your marketing plan, and there is some flexibility in which sites you use, how often you post, and the types of posts you make. So, use your creativity in designing your social media marketing, and most of all make it enjoyable for you and for your followers.

GET SET

CHAPTER 6

CREATING A MARKETING PLAN

A marketing plan not only helps you promote your book and build your brand, but it puts you in the mindset of being an author. The purpose of a marketing plan is simple: create discoverability of you and your book, get your book into the marketplace, and create interest so readers will buy it.

But you'd be surprised how many authors don't have a marketing plan. We see this time and again. If authors do not create a marketing plan, they flounder and marketing doesn't happen. The other scenario is marketing your book in a piecemeal manner, which usually isn't effective.

Marketing doesn't just happen. It needs to be planned and created on paper. Marketing your book will take time, planning, and patience. Your marketing plan is a reference guide of the items you need to do to market your book and a timeframe in which they should be done.

What Should Go In Your Marketing Plan

A marketing plan is unique and personalized for every author, but here are some of things you'll want to include in your plan/calendar for the year:

- How much time will you spend on social media? Will you do the postings, or will you hire someone to do it?

- How often will you update your website?

- When and how often will you buy marketing collateral?
- How often will you send out your newsletter?
- How often and when will you blog?
- What events do you plan to attend?
- Will you do book signings?
- Will you do a book tour? How long and in what areas?
- How often will you update your author profile on sites like Amazon and Goodreads?
- Will you do a book trailer? If so, when?
- How many marketing videos will you create, and where will you distribute them?
- When and where will you send in award program entries?
- Will you do giveaways and when?

The list above is just a sample of the items to consider as you create your marketing plan.

Where to Begin

A marketing plan doesn't have to be fancy or done in a certain format; it simply has to be effective for you. Here are some things to consider as you begin:

- Define your audience (who will most likely be interested in your book)
- Where can you find your audience (websites, events, etc.)
- Set your (realistic) goals for the year
- Set a yearly marketing budget
- Focus on discoverability (not selling)

- Create an elevator pitch (a thirty-second summary of your book if someone asks what it is about)

Every marketing plan is different, so it might be helpful to create a goal(s) of what you want to accomplish. The main goal is obvious: sell your book. But there are other smaller goals under that umbrella. As with anything, be reasonable. Chances are you won't be able to sell one thousand books in one month, but one hundred books in six months may be attainable.

First step

The first step in creating a marketing plan is to write down your ideas. As you sit down to create your marketing plan, don't get hung up on the format. Use whatever format works for you, whether it's putting pen to paper, using a bulleted Word or Pages document, or keeping track in an Excel spreadsheet.

The important thing is that the tasks or items you choose should eventually make their way to a calendar where you dedicate certain days and/or times to marketing. A marketing plan is simply creating a system whereby these things will get done on a regular basis. It needs to be in a format that is easy for you to follow.

Creating a Budget

You can't have a marketing plan without a budget. Some authors have a limited budget and will therefore have to concentrate their marketing on free things like social media posts or creating videos with their smartphones. Some authors will have a larger budget to attend events that have costs associated with them, or paying for advertising.

There are many resources available to guide you on how to make a budget, so please do your research or ask for help. When marketing a book, there are a few things you should consider for your budget:

- Website expenses
- Book purchase costs
- Travel expenses
- Help with social media postings
- Publicist (if you hire one)
- Event costs

It's important to update your marketing plan every year because the market changes and so do budgets. But remember, books do not have expiration dates. Keeping your book seen and relevant can help you have sales for many years.

Assess Your Strengths and Weaknesses

As we've identified, there are many aspects to book marketing, and you might not be able or interested in doing them all, so you may need outside help. Use your strengths and weaknesses to create and execute your marketing plan.

Make an honest assessment of your strengths. For example, maybe you love writing blogs. Some people are great with social media and have funny personas.

Then assess your weaknesses. Maybe you don't know how to build a website, or you're not confident when creating a budget. Your weaknesses may signal that you need to ask for help in those areas later down the road.

CHAPTER 7

THE INTERNET CAN BE YOUR BEST FRIEND

N ow that you understand the importance of marketing and developing a plan to consistently market, you may be feeling a bit overwhelmed. The good news is that in today's digital age, there are a myriad of marketing and learning tools available on the internet. You can learn so much from the World Wide Web, so it's important to become comfortable with doing internet searches.

Learning Tools

Use the internet to your advantage. If you are not familiar with something, look it up. Watch YouTube videos on how to create a book trailer. Attend webinars or online events to learn how to create a budget. Read books online from your library. The internet can provide a plethora of information, so don't be afraid to use it.

Marketing Ideas

The internet can be a great resource for developing your marketing plan. If you don't know where to begin, type "creating a book marketing plan" or "creating an author marketing plan" into your search engine and scan the information that pops up. These searches may open up opportunities or ideas that you hadn't thought of or haven't been mentioned in this book. Be open to discovering new ideas and technologies.

Learning from Other Authors

The internet is a great way to learn from other authors and to see what they are doing in terms of discoverability and book marketing. *Discoverability* means putting your author bio and book information in places where readers can find out about you and your book.

You probably already have favorite authors whose books you like to read. That's a good place to start. Now learn more about them and how they market.

- Look authors up on Amazon and read their profiles.

- Search for authors on the internet and see how many times their name comes up and from where that information originates.

- Find authors on social media sites and pay attention to what they post and where they post it.

- Look up authors' websites to see how they present themselves and what information they make available to readers and fans.

Looking up authors on Amazon

Amazon is an excellent website to discover up-and-coming authors or bestselling authors. We discuss the power of Amazon in chapter 9, but here is a quick explanation on how to find authors on Amazon.

- Go to Amazon's homepage and select Books from the drop-down menu.

- In the search bar, type in the name of the genre that you write in (e.g., mystery or romance).

- Scan down the list of books, then click on the books that interest you.

- Click on the author's name highlighted in blue, which will take you to the author's profile.

Once you have compiled information about other authors and how they market, you can use their approaches to perhaps expand or strengthen your own techniques.

The bottom line is to use the internet to your advantage. Don't be afraid to search and learn everything you can about book marketing from the different technologies available, or acknowledge how other authors are marketing themselves and their books.

CHAPTER 8

BOOK REVIEWS AND ENDORSEMENTS

F irst of all, it is important to understand the difference between a *review* and an *endorsement*. A review is from a reader or a fan. Endorsements are reviews that you receive from influencers such as authors, booksellers, educators, librarians, or experts in your field or genre. Endorsements are also called *editorial reviews,* which come from well-known reviewing companies like *Publishers Weekly* or *Kirkus Reviews.* Endorsements need to be acquired at least three or four months (or more) before your book is published, depending on your method of publishing and your publisher.

Benefits of Book Reviews and Endorsements

Book reviews and endorsements are important for many reasons:

- They let readers know what others think about your book.

- Endorsements give your book added credibility.

- Reviews can boost sales.

- Readers use book reviews or endorsements to help them decide what book to read or a new author they might want to start following.

- Quotes from reviews or endorsements can be used as part of your marketing.

  - You or your publisher can include quotes on the inside

of your book on a "praise" page as part of your book description or on other marketing materials.

Endorsements

To acquire an endorsement, your publisher will very likely send ARCs (advance review copy), Galleys (bound copies of your book before it is designed into an ARC or final copy), or PDFs of an ARC to reviewers.

The most well-known reviewers are:

- *Kirkus Reviews*
- *Publishers Weekly*
- *Library Journal*
- *The New York Times Book Review* (NYTBR)

You can also personally submit your ARC to reviewers (e.g. *Publishers Weekly* and *Kirkus),* but there is a cost for author submissions. Again, endorsements, especially one by a prominent reviewer, can give your book an added boost.

Acquiring Endorsements

There are a wide variety of places where you can submit your book for pre-publishing endorsements and you should solicit several. Aim to get at least five endorsements that can be printed on "praise" pages in the front interior of your book or uploaded to your profile page on places like Amazon.

Some of the entities from which you can solicit pre-publishing endorsements are:

- Magazines that focus on your genre
- "Big name" reviewers (*Kirkus Reviews, Publishers Weekly*, etc.)

- Local magazines or online magazines that do book reviews
- Newspapers
- Bloggers
- Websites that offer reviews

How to solicit endorsements

The ideal time for acquiring endorsements is when your book is in the ARC stage. The strongest endorsements can be inserted in the front of your book and used as promotions in your marketing campaign.

- If you have a publisher, find out what sources they reach out to for endorsements.

- If you are self-published, or if you want to reach out to an influencer your publisher is not reaching out to, find the source's review process (typically listed on their website) and follow it to the letter. If you don't follow their instructions, you are wasting your time and money.

- When sending your book to any reviewer, especially the larger ones, send it 14 to 16 weeks out from the pub date.

- Send your book with a cover letter and a page that includes the title, ISBN, release date, publisher, etc., along with any additional information they request. If you are unsure of how to put this information together, a quick search on the internet can give you some examples.

Getting ready to reach out

Research on how to acquire endorsements can help ensure your efforts are successful.

- To help you narrow down who you want to reach out to for

endorsements, make a list of authors, experts you admire and/or follow, and people who have endorsed books similar to yours. Narrow it down to 5 or 10 people that you want to reach out to.

- Once you've compiled your list, determine how you can connect with them.
- Find their website and look for a contact form.
- See if they list their email address in their books, on their website, or on their blogs.
- Look up their Google+ profile to check for an email address.
- Private message them through Facebook.
- Make an initial contact with them on Twitter.
- Plan ahead to give them at least 4 to 8 weeks' notice of your preferred deadline.
- Get creative in how you ask for an endorsement, but the most important step is to ask.

Follow up

- If someone agrees to do an endorsement for you, follow up 1 to 2 weeks before the deadline you gave. Often, a gentle reminder can be helpful and appreciated by those with hectic schedules.

Say "thank you"

- If someone does an endorsement for you, show your appreciation with a note and consider sending them an autographed print copy once your book is ready.

When you get an endorsement

- Put it on your website.

- Make it available to your editor and/or publisher for possible inclusion in the front of your book or on the cover.

- Put it out on social media.

- Add it to your Amazon profile under Editorial Reviews.

- Make sure your publisher is aware of the endorsement for their marketing purposes.

Reviews

Reviews are valuable marketing that you can post on your website, your Goodreads account, on Facebook, Twitter, Instagram, your newsletter, and on your blog. As mentioned earlier, reviews from readers typically happen after your book is published. Amazon will allow an author or publisher to post editorial reviews (endorsements) before a book is published, but reviews from readers will not be posted on their site until the book is released.

Bloggers as reviewers

- Search out bloggers who have a large audience of followers.

- Search out bloggers who write about and review books in your genre.

- Follow bloggers to get familiar with what they write about and the types of books they review.

- When submitting your book for a review, follow the submission guidelines.

- Book reviews don't have to stop once your book has been published or if it has been on the marketplace for a while. Look for bloggers who specialize in backlist books.

Readers as reviewers

Reviews that come from readers are important for the entire life of your book, and they are essential for building a fan base. Ask for reviews even after your book is in the marketplace or has been for some time. A review posted on social media can retrigger interest in your book, and reviews on your website can help trigger SEOs (search engine optimization) to get you listed in searches.

- Readers can post reviews of your books on Amazon, Goodreads, etc.

- Readers don't always think about posting reviews, so gently ask them or remind them via email, social media, etc.

- If someone has posted a review (Amazon, Goodreads, etc.), send them an email to thank them for taking the time to write a review.

NetGalley

NetGalley (www.netgalley.com) is a site that has been specifically designed for garnering reviews. Booksellers, librarians, reviewers, etc. are members of NetGalley and can download copies of your book from the site for reading and then reviewing.

Check to see if your publisher uses NetGalley. You can also upload your book to NetGalley as an author, but the cost can be high. If you are a member of IBPA (Independent Book Publishers Association) or other entities, you may be able to secure a discount.

Many reviewers will automatically put their review on Amazon or Goodreads. If they don't, you can reach out and ask them. If you receive a review via NetGalley before your book is published, you can upload it to your Amazon Author Profile in the Editorial Reviews section.

Reviews on Amazon

Reviews on Amazon are important for many reasons beyond the

fact that Amazon is one of the largest booksellers in the world. We dedicate an entire chapter to a discussion about Amazon in the next chapter.

CHAPTER 9

THE POWER OF AMAZON

A mazon is the biggest bookseller by far with a strong influence on consumers. When your book is listed on Amazon.com, it can also appear on a wide variety of Amazon sites in other countries.

If you self-publish your book, you will work directly with Amazon through an Amazon Central page where you can check inventory and sales of your book, as well as your author bio, videos, among other things. If you have a publisher, they will be in contact with Amazon regarding inventory, sales, etc., and your sales will be reported to you and paid to you via your publisher.

No matter how you are published, there are several things that you can do to help influence your book sales through Amazon.

Things to Know About Amazon

It is important to understand how Amazon works.

- Everything on Amazon is done via algorithms (computers), and books are automatically ordered when the demand is there.
- The pricing for books on their site is controlled by Amazon and is based on inventory levels, orders, competition, best-seller status, and promotions.
- Your book price on Amazon may vary from time to time; this is not unusual. However, the price that Amazon pays you (or

your publisher) remains the same based on your (or your publisher's) agreement with Amazon.

Amazon Reviews

Since Amazon is run via algorithms, reviews on their site are imperative to help trigger features like "readers who bought this, also bought this."

- People who buy in other places still look for reviews and author profiles on Amazon.

- Reviews on Amazon impact the number of your books they stock and act in triggering Amazon's marketing features.

- You need at least 10 reviews on Amazon for their algorithms to recognize your book.

- It takes 100 reviews on Amazon for all marketing features to kick in. (These numbers can change, but at the time of this writing, these are the minimum review numbers for features to kick in.)

Amazon Best Sellers

- The Amazon Best Sellers calculation is based on Amazon sales, clicks, etc. and is updated hourly to reflect recent and historical sales of every item sold on Amazon.

- An Amazon rating does not necessarily translate into huge dollar sales because it is based on the number of sales in that category.

- For instance, if you are rated number one in an obscure category that has 300 books in it, sales can be minimal.

- But the number-one rating still looks good and can be used on social media.

Videos

- Amazon is currently allowing publishers to upload one video per book on the Book Information page.
- Ask your publisher about providing a video for your book or if they are creating one.
- If you self-published, reach out to Amazon to see if this option is available for you.

A+ Content

Publishers can also create A+ Content for their Book Information page. These pages can include photos, award designations, etc.

The A+ pages can be found on the Book Information page in the From the Publisher section. Check with your publisher if they are creating A+ pages for your book. Self-published authors can connect with Amazon to discuss adding this feature to their book page.

Advertising Options

Amazon also offers advertising options, but make sure you research this thoroughly before you attempt to use them as they can quickly become very costly. In general, Amazon advertising is stronger for nonfiction books than for genre fiction.

Amazon Author Central

It is recommended to set up an Amazon Author Central page because this will activate your author name (create it as clickable) on your book page. From there, readers can access your author profile information.

When setting up your author profile on Amazon at https://authorcentral.amazon.com, remember to:

- Include your biography, photos, videos, links to social media, and links to your blog and/or upcoming events.

- Update your Amazon profile at least quarterly.

- Put the Amazon link (along with other retailer buy links) on your author website, your emails (under your signature), and social media accounts.

Amazon's Top Reviewers

Reviews in general can help sell your book, but the number of reviews you have on Amazon can help sell your book and trigger other marketing features.

One of the methods you can use to get more well-written and highly regarded reviews is to approach some of the Amazon Top Customer Reviewers. It will take time and research to find them and connect with them, but a review from one of the top reviewers can help escalate your sales. These reviewers have been identified by Amazon through Amazon's algorithms. A list of these reviewers can be found at https://www.amazon.com/reviews/top-reviewers.

- Scan through the list and identify reviewers who review books and not just products.

- Find book reviewers who review books in your genre or a similar genre.

- Send a reviewer an email about how you found them and why you think they'd be interested in your book.

- Follow their instructions for submitting your book to them.

- Offer them a free copy of your book. Many top reviewers are happy to discover new writers.

Amazon is a strong player in the world of marketing and selling books, so it is important to understand how the retailer works and utilize those features to get your book and your author information in front of readers all around the world.

CHAPTER 10

MARKETING VERSUS ADVERTISING

I t is important to understand the difference between *advertising, marketing,* and *selling.* The biggest misconception authors usually make is believing they have to be "good at selling" to succeed as an author. *But marketing isn't selling.* Marketing is letting the right group of people know about the ways your book will fill their needs, whatever those may be, and then where to purchase your book. And in order for that to happen, you need to be interested in discovering other people's needs.

In Dale Carnegie's book, *How to Win Friends and Influence People,* he asserted what everybody, in all situations, wants to know: "What's in it for me?" That statement holds true even stronger today than it did when Carnegie wrote his book in 1928. So, if all of your marketing is just about you, people will lose interest. The more your marketing offers something to people—laughter, information, entertainment, connection, etc.—the more it will draw people to you and to your book.

There are many ways to market your book, which have already been discussed in earlier chapters. The purpose of this chapter is to provide more details about other helpful marketing tools and to define advertising and when we recommend using it.

In-Person Events

In-person events can be a strong way to connect with people, build relationships, and promote your book. Here is a list of examples of in-person events that can help you market your book:

- Launch parties
- Book signings and readings
- Writers' conferences
- Book festivals
- Local events
- Bookseller events
- Speaking opportunities

Launch parties

Launch parties are generally held on the book's release date, or a few days before or after. The main purpose of a launch party is to celebrate the publishing of your book and to connect with your already-established fan base.

The number of books you should have on hand for your launch party will depend on how many people you expect. Generally, 30 to 50 percent of the people you invite will attend. And typically, 50 percent of those will buy your book.

- Themes of launch parties differ depending on your author brand and your book genre. There are lots of ideas online. It can be intimate or large.

- Bring a guest book and have everyone sign in with their email address to add to your email list for newsletters, blogs, etc.

- You can create a closed group on Facebook and invite friends from there. It can also be a good way to track attendance for your launch party.

- After the event, send thank-you notes or emails. Friends don't typically expect to be thanked, but the kind gesture goes a long way.

Book signings or readings

Book signings or readings can be a strong part of your marketing plan, so we have dedicated an entire chapter to this discussion. In chapter 12, we go into detail of how to find, pro-mote, and create book signings or readings.

Writers' conferences

There are writers' conferences of all sizes all around the country. A writers' conference is a good place to help market your book and enhance its discoverability. Remember, writers are readers too. If another writer likes your book, their word-of-mouth marketing about your book can be a strong addition to your marketing arsenal.

Again, the internet is your best source for discovering writers' conferences, both in your area and nationally. Make a list of the conferences that appeal to you, then narrow it down to those that fit into your budget and schedule.

Book festivals

Almost every state has a large book festival where authors and readers gather to be immersed in "everything books." At these festivals, there are tables and booths filled with books. There are also presentations on a variety of subjects and opportunities for readers to meet their favorite authors, to discover new authors, and for authors to expand their fan base.

Some of the larger book festivals are:

- The *Los Angeles Times* Festival of Books
- The Miami Book Fair
- The Carolina Mountains Literary Festival
- BookExpo America (held in New York City each year)

Writer's Digest also provides an online list of festivals that are held in each state. Please visit their website (https://www. writersdigest.com/publishing-insights/list-of-book-fairs-and-book-festivals-by-state) for more information.

Regional and community book festivals

There are also regional and community book festivals throughout the country that can be good opportunities to meet readers, other writers, and to display your book. Many festivals also offer opportunities for direct selling of your book to attendees.

- Search each festival website for the process they use to select the authors who present at the event, and, if appropriate for you and your book.

- If you are a new author, consider starting with smaller festivals to build experience and credibility.

- If you're an experienced author, consider applying to the larger events. Speaking at a book festival can create a big boost in your fan base and author name recognition.

Visit websites for the most up-to-date information.

Bookseller events

In chapter 17, we talk about bookseller associations and the events and marketing opportunities they offer, including their yearly conferences. As you decide which events you will participate in, read the information on these bookseller associations, and check out their websites to determine whether they are a good fit for your marketing plan.

Speaking opportunities

Not all authors want to speak to a group of people, but some are very comfortable with the idea. If you enjoy public speaking, this may be an area of marketing you want to develop. If you're a new author and relatively new to the speaking arena, it's likely you will not get paid for your first speaking gigs. As in all occupations, it is important to hone the craft and gain experience and credibility.

Here are some steps to develop your speaking opportunities:

- Develop a list of the topics you can speak about, from the process of writing to why you write what you do, etc.

- Start with local groups where you have a connection.

- Check out local writers' groups for opportunities.

- Explore book festivals (local, regional, and national).

- If you're a nonfiction author, explore industry events or business functions for speaking opportunities.

To reiterate: If you don't have experience as a speaker but want to develop that skill, start small, stay consistent in searching out opportunities, and go to events where other authors are speaking and learn by watching and listening to them. But most of all, have fun with the experience!

Marketing on Social Media

During the time of COVID-19, in-person marketing had to take a back seat, further emphasizing the importance of social media marketing and the power it can have in your marketing efforts. In chapter 5, we went into detail about building your social media platform. But in this section, we want to emphasize the importance of monitoring the messages that you are conveying in your social media marketing.

- Marketing is about building relationships and creating discoverability for your book, so periodically check your social media marketing to see what message you are conveying.

- Look at your posts over the last month to determine if you are only pushing your book. If so, create posts about other things that can showcase your persona.

- Pay attention to the posts that have gotten a lot of likes or comments. These are the posts that are resonating with the people who follow you.

If your social media marketing has gotten off-track, it is very easy to bring it back to where it needs to be.

Caring Can Be Marketing

To be successful in marketing your brand, it is important to look outward. The more authors reach out and contribute their skills, time, and knowledge, the more their brand and credibility are enhanced.

You can market, sharing your knowledge and helping others by:

- Contributing to web forums.

- Blogging about things that interest you other than writing and your book.

- Offering to write guest posts on someone else's blog.

- Read and review the works of other authors.

- Put a page on your website titled "Books I Love" (or something similar), and review the works of other authors you enjoy.

- Feature other authors on your social media.

- Use your blog to interview other authors.

- Attend book signings for authors you don't know, post about it, and tag the authors.

- Share your time for a cause you believe in.

- Be willing to share your expertise and knowledge by offering to do presentations at local groups, writers' workshops, etc.

Marketing Collateral

Marketing collateral can put your name, your book title, and the book cover in front of potential readers in a very nonintrusive way. Marketing collateral can be effective "walking billboards" for you and your book.

These are some of the most popular marketing collateral used by authors:

- Bookmarks (readers love bookmarks and are more likely to save them than they would a business card)

- Postcards

- Posters or signage for when you do presentations or book signings

- Announcement flyers for books signings

- Mugs or water cups

- Business cards (especially for business book authors)

- T-shirts that display your book cover and website URL

Advertising

Advertising is when you pay to have your book information put in front of people via print, social media, on the radio, or even on television (James Patterson uses the latter format a lot). There is a cost to advertising, and it is not something we generally recommend for new authors because the expense can escalate very quickly. If you are interested in advertising, make sure you explore your options to ensure that you will be reaching your target market (people who are most likely to buy your book).

The exception to this rule is social media advertising on sites like Facebook or Pinterest. Typically, their ads are low cost and can help expose your book to a larger audience. If social media advertising is of interest to you, take time to explore the option on Facebook or Pinterest. Each site has specific rules and options for advertising. The main focus is to ensure that the site gives you the opportunity to hone in on your target market.

CHAPTER 11

BOOKBUB

B ookBub is a site and email newsletters dedicated solely to promoting sales or giveaways of eBooks, and now audiobooks. BookBub got started from a newsletter that promoted free and on-sale eBooks to readers and by charging authors or publishers for listing their promotion.

BookBub has become a powerful force in the world of book marketing. It would benefit your book and author brand to be part of their platform.

Things to Know about BookBub

- Millions of people all over the world have an account with BookBub.

- When a reader signs up for the BookBub newsletter, they select their preferred genres. Then BookBub categorizes specific lists of readers based on their genre preferences and those readers are sent newsletters that focus on eBook sales and promotions of the genres they have selected.

- BookBub sends several targeted email newsletters each week covering different genres.

- Because BookBub separates their newsletters and reader lists into genres, an author is able to select specific promotions that focus on their target market.

- There are BookBub newsletters for the US market and for

the international market (Canada, Great Britain, Australia, New Zealand, etc.).

- Ads in a BookBub newsletter can get tremendous attention to a book.

- The category and territory of an ad is determined by Book-Bub.

- Prices for ads run from the hundreds to thousands of dollars depending on the genre category and the territory.

- Publishers or authors whose submissions are accepted for a BookBub promotion usually double or triple (or more) the investment they make by the sales they reap.

Become a BookBub Reader and Author

There are two ways to join BookBub: as a reader and as an author. It is important for authors to join BookBub as both a reader *and* an author to receive the most benefits. As a reader, you can follow your genre and keep up with new books that are releasing and deals that are being offered. As an author, you can create a following and build your brand.

As a BookBub reader, you can:

- Choose the genres you want to be notified about to eliminate "junk" information

- Receive emails about featured deals and new releases

- Follow friends to see what books they are interested in

- Follow your favorite authors or genres

- Get a list of authors under specific genres

- Post book reviews

- Create a booklist
- Buy your eBooks through BookBub links
- Support deals from your favorite authors

As a BookBub author, you can:

- Create an author profile
    - Add your photo
    - Add a biography
    - Add genres
    - Add a recently released or upcoming book
- Build a following
    - Recommend a book you love (this is a free way for authors to engage with readers)
    - Add a BookBub follow button to your website
    - Add a call-to-action ("follow me on BookBub") to your newsletter
    - Promote your BookBub Author Profile on your social media
    - Add a link "follow me on BookBub" to your email signature
    - Add a ClickToTweet link to your author profile bio to make it easy for your fans to share that they just followed you
- Use BookBub promotion opportunities to market your book
    - Set up preorder alerts
    - Run BookBub ad campaigns to promote your profile
    - You or your publisher can create BookBub ads

- You or your publisher can submit your book for a Featured New Release, which is a promotion through Book-Bub's newsletter

- Have a Partners Dashboard to place ads and featured deals

- Follow the Partners Blog that offers marketing information

Building a following on BookBub as an author can help you build your author brand as well as your fan base because BookBub has a target audience of readers. Once you are set up as an author on BookBub, your followers will get notified by BookBub for a new release, a preorder alert, or a discount.

Backlist Titles on BookBub

Not only is BookBub important for new releases, but it is crucial to keep your account active for backlist titles.

- Be an active author by recommending other books and authors.

- Consider a BookBub ad (pay per click) every three to four months.

- Follow other authors of your genre on BookBub.

- Promote the dickens out of your new releases and have backlist titles linked to them.

- Promote your BookBub Author Profile on your social media to keep pushing new readers to your books.

BookBub has marketing opportunities that are always expanding and changing. Make the BookBub website one of your favorites and go to it often as an author to participate in the many opportunities they offer. Work with your publisher to find out how they use BookBub and which ways they recommend you use it. If you are self-published, BookBub can be one of your strongest marketing tools.

CHAPTER 12

BOOK SIGNINGS OR READINGS

B ook signings or readings are an important part of an ongoing marketing plan and can be crucial in helping authors continue to build a fan base and their author brand. That said, these types of events are not always easy to set up because bookstores are often deluged with authors who want access to their customers. It has to be financially beneficial for a bookstore to tie up their time and space for an author to come into the store.

Setting up book signings and/or readings will most likely be your responsibility. If you are with a larger publisher, they may have someone on staff to assist with the efforts. But if you are with a smaller publisher or are self-published, it will be up to you. This chapter provides guidance on how to go about setting up a book signing or reading.

Marketing is about connecting with readers, bookstores, and other authors. But it doesn't just magically happen. As mentioned in chapter 5, having a strong social media presence will help you create your platform to gain a following. But you can't only live online. Successful authors participate in events, which can help build awareness.

Setting up Book Signings or Readings

Book signings are an excellent way to meet-and-greet the public while selling your book! If your books are traditionally distributed, setting up a book signing should be relatively easy. Your books will be in all databases for chain stores and independent bookstores for quick ordering.

But if you are not a well-known author, it may be difficult to set up a book signing or reading. It is important to work on developing relationships with your local bookstores.

Approaching bookstores

- Make a list of the booksellers (or other retailers) with whom you would like to do a book signing and/or reading.

- Before you approach a bookstore, learn about them. Sign up for their newsletter if they have one. Find out how many readings they do a month, or what other events they host. (story times, book clubs, etc.) How would you and your book fit into their ongoing schedule?

- Most stores will have a "local author" section and often designate one or two days a year for "local author signings," which can give you an opportunity to get your book in front of the bookstore.

- Meet the person in charge of events and express your interest in participating.

- If you visit in person, bring them a press kit.

- Get an ARC (Advance Review Copy) of your book to your local bookstores as soon as the copies are available.

- If your book has traditional distribution, your book should be in their database and system. Many bookstores order through Ingram or via Edelweiss. Find out from your publisher if your books are in either or both systems.

- If you are a new author, sometimes retailers' databases (especially through Ingram distribution) will show only one or two copies in stock. The bookstore should be able to request additional copies from the distributor or wholesaler for a book signing. Or, you can reach to your publisher to request that Ingram put more books in stock for a particular event.

- If you are self-published, make sure booksellers know that. As a self-published author, expect a little resistance, but inquire if they have "local author" events in which you could participate.

- If you are a new author, you may encounter some resistance in the beginning. Don't get discouraged.

Links and reviews

- IndieBound is a website where independent bookstores can group together for marketing. If you are going to work with independent bookstores, it is imperative that you have a Buy Link for your book to IndieBound.org on your website. Many indie stores won't do a book signing with you if you don't have an IndieBound link on your website. Info on how to get an Indie Bound link can be found at http://www.indiebound. org/spread-word

- Use reviews or testimonials from other booksellers in the press kit you present to the bookseller.

- Use NetGalley reviews from booksellers in your presentation materials.

Planning

- Books generally have to be in stock in the store before they'll do an event. Indie stores often use a local author showcase area to get new authors on their shelves.

- Tell the bookstore if your book is in the local libraries.

- A bookstore may be interested in carrying your book even though they may ask you to provide the books and they will carry them on consignment.

- Books should be no more than six months old for most bookstores to want to do an event unless something has happened with your book or with you that is helping to drive interest.

After booking the event

- When you do an event with a bookstore, help promote your event. If you can help drive traffic to the bookstore, they will notice and will want to have your book on their shelves.

- Once you work with a bookseller and establish good rapport, ask if they would be willing to give you a review.

- Don't set up a lot of events in different bookstores in a small area—that defeats your purpose. There are only so many customers in a geographical area, and more than one event in the same timeframe dilutes the possible traffic that could be generated for a store.

Promote your book signing

- What type of marketing does the bookstore allow? Will you be able to live stream the event from the bookstore?

- Do you have a strong following in the area from which you can attract attendance to your book signing?

- Promote the signing with social media, on your blog, etc.

- Some bookstores or entities will let you create a poster for their window.

- Some entities will let you create flyers that you provide to them to hand out to customers, to put into bags with purchases, etc.

- If you have super fans or a street team, get them involved in helping you promote your event.

Create a successful book signing or reading

Once you've set up a book signing or reading, the work has just begun. Make sure you communicate with the bookstore to find out how they are going to promote the signing or reading and share your plans for promotion. Keep in mind that most bookstores are expecting the authors to strongly promote the event and bring new customers into their store.

- Go prepared
  - The store usually provides the table, so consider bringing a tablecloth for a better presentation.
  - Bring accessories to make the table look festive.
  - Have an easel and author poster to set behind, beside, or on the table (depending on the size).
  - Come prepared with a pen that writes well and will make an impressionable signature.
- Get there early.
- Interact with people—don't just sit behind the table expecting people to come to you.
- Don't just push your book, build relationships. Be ready to talk with people, and not just about your book. Remember, people buy from people they like, so be likeable.
- Understand that you are there to build your fan base and that's what will sell your books.
- Hand out bookmarks to everyone who attends a reading or who stops at your table.
- Readers will want to know how to follow you after the event,

so ensure that your website and social media URLS are on your bookmarks.

- Don't be "in their face" about buying your book. Build your author brand and fan base by being approachable, nice, and someone they'd like to know.
- If the event includes a reading, be available and accessible after the reading to talk with people, sign your books, etc.

The more books you sell, the more the bookstore will want you to come back, and the more book signings you set up, the easier it will be to get more book signings.

How Libraries Can Help

While libraries don't typically produce a lot of revenue for authors, they can help create strong visibility. Libraries can help communities learn about local authors and their books. Building a relationship with the librarians at your local libraries can create discoverability of your book and open up appearances and speaking events in your area.

Consider donating a copy of your book to libraries in your area or in an area where your book takes place. Donating one copy can lead to more copies being purchased to keep in the library. Be willing to donate to all types of libraries: public, school, university. If your local libraries sponsor events and giveaways are part of the event, consider donating copies of your book for the giveaway.

CHAPTER 13

BUILDING YOUR FAN BASE

R eaders who diligently follow you and your books become a part of your fan base. The best way to turn readers into fans is to grab them with your profiles on Amazon, Goodreads, and BookBub. Gather them together in a Facebook group or with signups to your newsletter. Once you've gathered them, share information such as great Amazon rankings, appearances, events, or promotions. Show some love by encouraging feedback or addressing concerns. Behind every successful author is a loyal fan base.

Building a loyal fan base can take time and patience, but the rewards are worth it. There are many ways that readers can discover you:

- BookBub

- Social media

- Recommendations from friends and family

- Recommendations from authors they follow

- Facebook author groups

- Partner with relevant local organizations

    - Children's/YA authors coordinate with local schools or PTAs to appear at events.

    - For a sci-fi book, host a signing at a sci-fi convention.

- If your story takes place at a particular location, run a promotion with that location.

Facebook and Fans

It's no secret how influential Facebook can be in the budding career of a new author. As discussed throughout this book, social media plays such an important role in how we communicate our message, and Facebook is a perfect platform for gaining new fans.

Here are a few ways you can use Facebook to your advantage:

Create reader communities

Launch a Facebook group with other authors to announce new releases, hold monthly joint giveaways, etc.

- Host Facebook Q&A sessions

  - Create an event on Facebook and send invitations to your followers.

  - Remind guests who receive RSVP notifications of the event as the date approaches.

- Host a Facebook Live chat

  - Reveal the inspiration for a book.

  - Show a sneak peek of an upcoming release.

  - Reveal the title of an upcoming release.

  - Reveal the cover of an upcoming release.

  - Introduce new characters.

  - Announce a book's release date.

  - Ask your fans for ideas on what you should write your next book about.

- Create a pre-recorded video where you answer fan's questions.

Build a Street Team

One of the fastest ways to gain recognition as an author is to gather your fans into what is called a "street team." A street team is a group of people who gladly spread the word about you and your book. Some authors use Facebook groups to organize their street teams and recruit new members.

Feeling overwhelmed? Street team members might be able to assist you in managing your social media pages depending on their strengths. Some might be able to update your website. You'd be surprised at how involved some members want to become to help you get more recognition.

Create a street team

- Invite people to help you share information about you and your book.

- Ask for help (i.e., social media posts, handing out bookmarks, etc.).

- Your team can share things both virtually and literally. Word of mouth is a strong marketing tool!

- Draw on your team's strength.

Yes, it can be scary to begin asking for help, but do it anyway. Once you get started, you'll find that your street team will help motivate and inspire you. Here are some of things your street team can do for you.

- Post reviews of your book (on Amazon, Goodreads, etc.)

- Share information about you and your book on their social media account(s)

- Distribute swag (bookmarks, pens, etc.) to potential readers
- Pitch one of your books at their library or local bookstores (chain or indie)

Engage with your street team

There should be benefits to being part of your street team aside from being a fan of your writing. Some of the things you can do for your street team are:

- Send Advance Review Copies (ARC) of your upcoming books
- Send notes to thank them for reading
- Invite them to review your book
- Value them and they will value you

Super Fans versus Street Teams

Have you heard of the Beyhive or the Swifties? These are a legion of super fans for Beyoncé and Taylor Swift, respectively. While authors may not have the same reputation as a pop star, they can still have loyal super fans (ahem, George R. R. Martin).

The difference between super fans and a street team is that super fans—while they love what you do and buy your books—do not actively engage or "hit the streets" to help promote you and your books. Street teams do.

Super fans

- Love everything you do
- Buy all of your books
- Give social media love to your posts
- Comment on your blog

Street team

- Follows your requirements to be a part of your street team

- Actively engages in your success
- Willingly shares your stuff
- Helps promote you
- Shares on social media
- Blogs
- Posts event info nearby
- Has a clear schedule and executes it

How to Grow Your Super Fans

- Offer free books
- Offer exclusives (i.e., the first chapter of a new book)
- Write newsletters
- Share offers

Turning Your Super Fans into Street Teams

- Email your list and invite them to participate.
- Reward them (send gift cards, handwritten notes, swag, etc.).
- Spend time with them via social media, or if they are close, set up personal interactions, when possible.

Keeping an active, effective street team requires time and attention in the form of interaction and creating special opportunities for them. Readers become part of a street team because they have the opportunity to build a special relationship with an author they enjoy. Remember, it is human nature to think, "What's in it for me?" and that applies to street teams as well. The more interaction and special "goodies" they receive from an author they like, the more they will be willing to do to help promote you and your book.

CHAPTER 14

PUBLICITY

Publicity is everything from interviews online or in magazines, articles, radio interviews, television interviews, etc. Some authors are equipped to do their own publicity and others are not. Either way, please understand that publicity is important, and being able to step outside the box in creating publicity is a strong component in helping you be successful.

Publicity is about using various sources, contacts, and means to create a buzz and fan base for your book and creating a brand for you as an author. At one time, publicity was completely centered around the media and getting media coverage (print, radio, television). Now, social media provides a broad scope for interacting with potential readers, building a relationship with readers, and giving readers more access to you than an article in a magazine, an hour on the radio, or a brief television interview ever could.

The first step in designing the publicity part of your marketing plan is determining if you can and want to create your book publicity, or if you would rather hire a publicist. In this chapter, we provide some tips on how to make that decision.

What Does a Publicist Do?

Unless you are published by a large publisher and they expect to make a lot of money with your book, hiring a publicist or doing your own publicity will generally fall on your shoulders. A word of caution: money can quickly disappear when publicity is being created without you actually knowing where it has gone. Publicity and publicists don't and can't promise results. Publicists work to create opportunities for you and your book. Some of those opportunities will come to fruition, but others won't yield anything. Some will produce sales, some won't.

Each publicist or publicist group has their own set of possibilities, but if you are interested in hiring a publicist, make sure you are dealing with someone who specializes in book marketing, as there are specifics for book marketing that don't pertain to other areas of marketing.

A book publicist can do a number of things to help you promote your book:

- Devise and execute a book platform
- Help create author branding
- Acquire endorsements
- Create buzz strategies
- Procure placements on TV, radio, in print, with bloggers, etc.
- Develop ad copy
- Coordinate events
- Set up book reading tours
- Help with award applications
- Help design book trailers
- Create a strategy for a book blog
- Assemble a media kit
- Pitch interviews and features
- Plan the book launch event and book talk
- Schedule, host, and promote the book's virtual tour
- Position the title to booklists

- Formulate the author's talking points for presentations
- Recommend venues with high-traffic author events
- Leverage the interest of special audiences and book groups

Should you hire a publicist?

When you learn about what a publicist can do for you, you may decide to hire one. But it's important to understand that there are also risks involved (financially or otherwise).

- Generally, publicists charge from $2,000 to $5,000 per month with a three-month minimum contract.
- There is no guarantee of results.
- There are good publicists and not so good ones.
- If you decide to hire a publicist, ask for references from authors they have represented.

How to Become Your Own Publicist

Publicists focus on getting attention for the author they are representing. Buzz strategies get people talking about you and your books. There are a variety of tools that publicists use to "get a buzz going."

Creating buzz strategies

- Encourage communication through social networks and website forums.
- Make communication simple with information that can easily be shared or forwarded and will inspire people to share what they saw or experienced.
- Establish blogs and a social media presence and contribute to them on a regular basis.

- Engage in conversation with readers and fans through social media, blogs, etc.
- Identify influential people and connect with them through social media, forums, etc.
- Connect with people through user groups, fan clubs, message boards, etc.

The whole purpose is to "get the word out" about you and your book in a way that will create an interest and inspire people to follow you, and to spread the word about who you are and what you write.

Devise and execute your book platform

An author platform is simply all the ways you are visible and appealing to your future, potential, or actual readership. A platform is your "tribe" that consists of groups or communities of interest that are a part of your ideal readership.

- Author blogs
- Writing forums
- Other people's blogs
- Facebook groups and pages
- LinkedIn discussion groups
- Twitter discussions and lists
- Social media groups
- Any speaking you do
- Classes you teach
- Public appearances you make

Build and/or enhance your brand

You learned in chapter 2 how to create your author brand. By this point, you should know how important it is to not only build but also maintain your author brand. It is recommended to review your brand periodically to ensure that it represents you as an author in the most effective, powerful way.

Acquire endorsements

Endorsements can help propel your book to success and help build a fan base that is strong and powerful. (See chapter 8 about the importance of reviews and endorsements.)

Getting media attention

Media attention covers a large span, from appearing on television or radio programs to having articles or interviews in newspapers, magazines, or with bloggers. Before you go after media attention, be very honest with yourself as to what you will be comfortable with. Many authors feel comfortable giving interviews for newspapers, magazines, or with bloggers, but the idea of being on the radio or television makes them break out into a sweat. That's okay. If it doesn't work well for you, then don't do it. But if you're just a little nervous because you've never done it before, then you may just need to push yourself a tad to acquire the experience.

Getting placements in the media

An article in a magazine, an interview on a radio or a podcast, or an appearance on a television talk show can be a huge boost in creating discoverability for your book. These things in and of themselves will not necessarily boost sales, but they can trigger interest in your book, word-of-mouth endorsements, and other publicity opportunities.

Getting these placements is not as easy as it sounds, and it requires planning and follow-through. The suggestions on the next page can get you started on this endeavor.

• Create a media list

- Your target TV programs, radio programs, publications, reporters, bloggers

• Determine the topics or angles you can pitch to your target list

- Find creative ways to talk about yourself as an author and your book

• Connect with reporters, TV personalities, bloggers, etc. via social media

- Follow them and begin to create a relationship

- Add new media contacts to your list as you discover them

• Attend events where you can meet key contacts

• Use the list whenever you have news to share

- A new release

- An award

- A significant appearance (keynote speaker, etc.)

• Use Google alerts or other methods to help notify you when your book, your name, or a topic your book covers are being talked about in the media (https://www.google.com/alerts)

Getting interviews on radio, podcasts, or local television shows

Talk shows that air locally via radio, podcast, or television can be a good way for authors to get attention in their local areas, which can lead to broader coverage. But for the shows to consider giving you airtime, you need to have some interest beyond the fact that you've published a book. So do your research.

Getting on the air

• Find local radio shows, podcasts, or television shows that are popular in your area.

- What types of interviews do they do, and have you heard or seen them interview authors? If so, what types of authors?
- Pay attention to the types of shows they do so you can pitch ideas according to their trends.
- Find out whom to contact.
- Once you have the contact information, reach out either via email or regular mail.
- Email, send, or drop off a professional author press kit in person. Include a listing of any local events (speaking events, book signings, etc.) that you have planned.

You're on the air

- If you book a television appearance, make sure you are prepared by dressing the part. Look professional!
- Provide a list of interview questions for the host.
- Bring a copy of your book.
- Provide a website URL and/or a list of where your book can be purchased. If they have this information, some of it might be posted on the screen during your appearance.
- Podcasts are often done via Zoom, so prepare the space from which you'll broadcast and ensure that your speakers, video, and lighting are all set up. Also, dress the part.
- Radio shows are typically done via phone or Zoom (without the video), so prepare your space to be as quiet as possible so there will be no sound interference.

Create an Online Media Kit

A main tool for the media is called a *media kit*. This kit typically contains:

- A press release
- Contact information
- A book blurb
- Photos of you and your book
- Your bio
- Top reviews of your book
- Excerpts from your book
- Links to where your book can be purchased

If you are unsure of how to create a media kit, you can find templates online. Once you have a kit created, it's important to have it available to hand out to bookstores or people you contact in person. Also, have it available on your website (and/or blog) where it is easy to find (i.e., a link that says, "download media kit"). A reporter, bookstore, etc. can then access all components of your media kit with a click of a link.

Extend the Life of Your Media Coverage

Getting media attention is good exposure, so you'll want to capitalize on that exposure. Don't let an interview fade into the background after six months. We suggest boosting posts every so often to keep things fresh.

- Every time your book is featured, or you are interviewed, turn those into their own blog post.
- Share behind-the-scenes photos, footage, or anecdotes from television or radio appearances or interviews.
- At the end of each year (or month if you get a lot of publicity), create a slideshow of media highlights and milestones that you can feature on your website and post on your social media.

Setting up Events

One of the biggest projects that a publicist can do for an author is setting up events. If you plan to be your own publicist, you will need to seek out events, know how to set them up, and how to execute them.

The first step is to seek out events and venues that would be appropriate for you as a person and author. Now, there is a little "selling" in that you'll have to convince the event director or coordinator that you are a good fit for what they are trying to do.

Some good sources for event or appearance possibilities are:

- Book festivals (both national and local)
- Bookseller conferences
- Bookstore events
- Library events
- Book clubs
- Reading groups
- Schools
- Business events
- Nonprofits
- Causes you believe in

Please note that when a publicist is searching out and setting up events, they are focused on building your brand and your fan base, not selling books. Once a brand and fan base are built, the book sales will follow.

Organizing a Book Tour

Once you have organized and set up several events, you may be able to turn those events into a book tour and fill in with local events in the areas where you will be visiting. Keep in mind that a book tour does take a lot of planning, especially depending on how far you travel, and you will need to budget for any expenses.

Where to begin

- Create a timeframe for your tour.
- Allow a two- to three-month lead time for setting up events.
- Decide on the geographical area of your tour.
- Designate the cities and/or towns you want to consider.
- Create a budget for travel expenses (gas, food, hotels, etc.).
- Make a list of the bookstores/events that you'd like to do.
- Contact venues.
- Send out author press kits and a copy of your book to the venue along with a letter that expresses your interest.
- Place follow-up calls to bookstores/venues.

Working with your budget

Book tours can be expensive if you are planning to stay in hotels, B&Bs, or Airbnbs each night. That's great if you have the budget for it, but don't let a limited budget stop you from doing a book tour if that is something you want to do. Get creative.

Here are a few suggestions:

- Plan your tour around areas where you have friends or relatives that you can stay with to cut down on hotel costs.
- Some authors have motorhomes or travel trailers they take on tour.
- Be adventurous! Camp at local campgrounds and bring your family on tour with you. While they're enjoying the campground, you can go off to your book signing or reading.

- Plan book tours around family vacations to combine some book marketing with having a great time with your family and exploring new areas.

Plan your travel itinerary

A successful book tour depends on having a solid itinerary before you begin, but also being willing to be flexible once the tour is in full swing. For instance, an opportunity may arise to do a book signing in a small town close to one of the stops on your itinerary. See if you can work it in. Perhaps you'll do two book signings in one day instead of just the one you had planned.

On the road

When your tour begins, contact book-oriented radio shows, newspaper lifestyle sections, and alternative weeklies along the way. Some types of media typically need just a few days' notice.

- Pitching to TV shows in the different areas you will be visiting will need to be done well in advance.
- Use social media to promote your events.

SUCCEED!

CHAPTER 15

FINDING SUCCESS AS AN AUTHOR

W hat does success as an author look like to you? Have you defined it? Do you want to be a bestselling author, or do you have other goals that will define that term for you?

Whatever your definition of being a successful author is, you must be an active author to achieve success. That means you must have an active marketing plan and continue to work your plan. You can't publish your book and then sit back and do nothing, hoping your book will sell. Successful authors really live the role. They market, they engage, they continue writing.

Becoming a successful author takes time. Going from newly published to a great success overnight is a myth. Success, however you define it, is a long-term goal that needs to be pursued on an ongoing basis. And this can be a challenge because enthusiasm can wane when you feel like you are continually doing the same thing week after week and year after year. It can be very easy to slip into a routine where your marketing plan continues to look the same. The reality is that continuous marketing is essential, but you must mix it up to create long-term success.

Keep it Interesting

An important part of keeping marketing interesting is thinking outside of the box. Set up a time each year to look at your marketing plan and add some different options that you hadn't done the year before. Perhaps you've gained enough confidence and you now want to try speaking events or presentations where in the past you've shied away from them. If you don't yet have a street team, maybe it's time to create one. Finding success as an author requires ongoing effort from you, but it should also be fun.

Freshen up Your Marketing Efforts Each Year

If you haven't tried some of these yet, you might want to consider adding one or more to your marketing plan:

- Create a book trailer with specific software or by using your smartphone. Book trailers or other videos can be hosted on your website or on YouTube.

- Are you blogging? If not, it might be time to do it. If you are blogging, make sure your blog is current and up to date. Is your blog connected to your website and your author profile on Amazon?

- Set up guest blogs for other bloggers or websites that would attract your market.

- Do a presentation. You can start with local organizations or a local Meetup group.

- Give a talk at a local school or business club if your content is appropriate for the group.

- Consider hosting a discussion group. There are several websites on which discussion groups can be hosted. Search the internet to see if they are a good match.

- Participate on a podcast. Even if your book was published several years ago, come up with some relevant topics you can speak on and find podcasts that would be a good match.

- Do an eBook signing. Backlist titles work well for eBook

signings, especially if your book has currently won an award or is relevant to a trending topic. There are sites that will guide you and help you host one.

• If you are an author of a young adult or children's book, doing school events or readings at school can be a productive and effective marketing tool and they can be fun to do.

• Homeschooling groups are often looking for online events to include as part of their curriculum. If your book is appropriate for school-age children, consider reaching out. For information on homeschooling groups in your area, check out http://homeschoolcentral.com/support/index. htm.

• Put some fun into your marketing by finding a little known holiday and create a campaign or online event around one. Social media is a great place to do this. Check www. holidayinsights.com

• If you have nonfiction books that would sell well to companies or associations, check out:

  - www.manta.com to find a list of different types of businesses

  - www.weddles.com/associations to find lists of different types of associations

  - http://officialcitysites.org to obtain information about city contact information

• Technology is consistently changing and offering new opportunities and ideas, which can keep marketing interesting. Become an internet search junkie, seeking out a new approach or a new concept that you can integrate into what you already do.

Congratulate Yourself along the Way

As business owners, we often focus on the bottom line instead of taking time to celebrate our achievements along the way. As an author, it is imperative to congratulate yourself when you hit important milestones. Here are some examples:

- Your book sells 100 copies
- Your first book signing event
- The first award your book receives
- Your first royalty check
- And the list goes on . . .

Important milestones will differ for each author, but these milestones are an important part of recognizing your success as an author.

Finding Success

Finding success as an author is about meeting your goals and about what success means to you. Not all of us have the desire to be a bestselling author and that's okay. The important part of finding success as an author means identifying what that means to you and then recognizing it when it happens.

Success doesn't happen overnight. It takes long-term commitment and dedicated attention to create success. And it requires regular assessment of what you're doing, what's working, what's not working, and where you need to make changes to continue toward achieving your goal.

CHAPTER 16

BOOK CLUBS AND READING GROUPS

Book clubs and reading groups are all about reading and discovering books. Your book doesn't have to be a new release to attract a book club. These groups can be great discoverability tools for getting your book into the hands of more readers. In today's publishing environment, connecting with readers is paramount to success, and book clubs and reading groups are a great way to do that. Plus, word-of-mouth is one of the strongest tools that authors have, and book clubs and reading groups can start that chatter.

Many well-known authors have kicked up their awareness through book clubs, and even bestselling authors continue to engage with book clubs on an ongoing basis. It doesn't matter if your book has been out a few weeks or several years—approach book clubs and reading groups and sell them on why your book would be a relevant or entertaining read.

Finding and Approaching Book Clubs

Almost every community has book clubs, from those that are associated with bookstores to local groups of friends that gather, to larger groups that are formed through meetups. Book clubs love authors, and authors need book clubs because they provide direct connection with readers. Book club reads are generally shared more often than a book a reader will read on their own. Once an author has impacted a book club with one book, the book club and/or book club members tend to read all of that author's work.

Finding book clubs

- Ask your friends and acquaintances
- Check out local bookstores or coffee shops where book clubs often meet
- Search for book clubs on Facebook and Goodreads
- Search online for book clubs in your city
- Check out Meetup for book clubs (http://bookclub.meetup. com) in your area
- Use relevant hashtags on your social media (i.e. #ColoradoBookClubs)

Contacting book clubs

Before you contact a book club, make sure you've done your research and know the type of books they read. If they don't read your genre, don't waste their time and yours. Some book clubs review books for entertainment, while others read and review nonfiction books for information.

Once you've researched the club

- Contact the organizer to introduce yourself.
- Provide a book description.
- Explain that you're interested in participating as a visiting author, either in person or virtually.
- Explain where they can find your book—if it's available through the library, for purchase on your website, or if it's available at a discount if bought in bulk.

Keep in mind that book clubs often plan their reading lists months in advance, so don't expect a quick turnaround from your connection to your visit.

Approaching a book club

- How does your book stand out from other books of the same genre?
- How is your protagonist different?
- How is your story different?
- If your book is a nonfiction book, what information does it provide?

Pitching to book clubs

- Develop connections before you pitch.
- Make sure the club reads your genre.
- Create a list of questions as a handout, as well as on your website.
- Be kind and willing to visit either in person or via Skype, Facebook, etc.
- Don't do a hard-sell push. Create a relationship where they will want to read your book.

Invited to a book club

- Be on time.
- If it is a virtual visit, make sure you understand the program that you will be using and make sure your computer is set up and ready to go.
- Decide if you want to prepare a list of discussion points or speak on the fly.

- If you prepare discussion points, provide the list to the organizer before the event.

- If you want to speak on the fly, still be prepared to discuss certain topics. Knowing what you want to discuss can prevent moments of awkward silence.

- Be ready to ask questions and engage the readers. Ask what they liked about the book or what didn't work for them. Be ready to receive both praise and criticism. If it's criticism, don't take it personally or try to change their mind. Just accept what comes and enjoy the experience.

- Whether or not someone liked your book, they can walk away really having enjoyed their interaction with you and have pleasant memories and comments about you as an author.

- Bring bookmarks for everyone attending. If you do a virtual event, you can send the bookmarks ahead of time to the organizer to pass out to those attending.

- If in person, offer to sign copies of your book.

- Remember to kindly ask if they would consider leaving a review of your book on Goodreads and on Amazon (if they purchased your book from Amazon).

Finding Library Reading Groups

Most libraries have groups of people who gather to read a book and discuss it. Many of them also offer opportunities to authors to appear in front of the groups for questions and interactions. Library reading groups read books from all genres: fiction, nonfiction, children's, young adult, business books, self-help books, etc.

- Connect with local libraries about their reading groups,

what genres they read, and how you can get your book considered for a group.

- Search the internet for library reading groups in your area, then find the person in charge and connect.

CHAPTER 17

BOOKSELLER ASSOCIATIONS

There are nine bookseller associations across the country that support the independent bookstores in their regions. Their websites, newsletters, and annual conferences provide information that can help booksellers run and promote their individual bookstores.

The associations also provide marketing opportunities for publishers and authors to get their book information out to booksellers, which can be a strong marketing tool. If a bookseller likes a book or becomes a fan of a particular author, they will promote that book or author in their bookstore.

Publishers and authors can become members of a bookseller association with a yearly membership fee. Each organization offers different opportunities with the membership fee, from providing a list of bookseller contact information, to reduced advertising costs, or opportunities to speak at or exhibit at their annual conferences.

Bookseller Associations

The following is a list of the nine bookseller associations and the states they cover. Please note: some states are covered under duplicate organizations depending on the area of the state. Each association has membership opportunities for publishers and individual authors. Check with your publisher about which bookseller association they belong to, as this will help you determine whether individual membership will be beneficial.

Great Lakes Independent Booksellers Association
  (GLIBA): http://www.gliba.org
    - Minnesota, Wisconsin, Illinois, Indiana, Ohio, Michigan, Kentucky

Midwest Independent Booksellers Association
  (MIBA): http://midwestbooksellers.org
    - Illinois, Iowa, Kansas, Michigan, Minnesota, Missouri, Nebraska, North Dakota, South Dakota, Wisconsin

Mountain & Plains Independent Booksellers Association
  (MPIBA): http://www.mountainsplains.org
    - Arizona, Colorado, Kansas, Montana, Nebraska, Nevada, New Mexico, Oklahoma, South Dakota, Texas, Utah, Wyoming

New Atlantic Independent Booksellers Association
  (NAIBA): https://www.newatlanticbooks.com
    - New York, New Jersey, Pennsylvania, Delaware, DC, Maryland, Virginia, West Virginia

New England Independent Booksellers Association
  (NEIBA): https://www.newenglandbooks.org
    - Connecticut, Maine, Massachusetts, Metro Boston, New Hampshire, New York, Rhode Island, Vermont

Northern California Independent Booksellers Association
  (NCIBA): http://www.nciba.com
    - Northern California

Pacific Northwest Booksellers Association
(PNBA): http://www.pnba.org
- Alaska, Idaho, Montana, Oregon, Washington

Southern California Independent Booksellers Association
(SCIBA): http://www.scibabooks.org
- Southern California

Southern Independent Booksellers Alliance
(SIBA) http://www.sibaweb.com
- Alabama, Arkansas, Florida, North Carolina, South Carolina, Georgia, Kentucky, Louisiana, Mississippi, Tennessee, Virginia, West Virginia

Each association varies in what they offer. Most publishers are associated with one or several of the associations and participate in events or marketing. These are some of the examples of what the different organizations offer:

- All associations have yearly trade shows where publishers can exhibit and promote their books.

- Each association offers advertising opportunities in their catalogs.

- Several of the associations offer book award programs.

- Several offer special author programs to put authors and indie bookstores together.

- Some of the associations offer an "Authors on tour" calendar where an author can list any tours they have planned.

If you join an association as an author, here are a few of benefits they provide:

- Training and tips on how to market your book to independent booksellers.

- Author speaking opportunities at trade shows.

- NEIBA offers a "Book Alert" program that gets free review copies of forthcoming titles to buyers and frontline booksellers in their region.

- SIBA offers free membership to authors who place a "Find an Indie Bookstore" badge above the fold on the homepage of their website.

- Mail or email lists for all of the bookstores that are part of their membership. You can use these lists as the foundation for your own marketing plan.

- GLIBA offers a "Regional Access Program" for books with a regional interest.

- MIBA has a "Midwest Connections" program.

- NAIBA gives authors who join their association a page on their website and one free profile in the NAIBA newsletter.

Please note that the benefits listed above were accurate as of the writing of this book, but programs and offerings can and do change. For an accurate listing from each association, please visit their website.

Ways You Can Participate

Regional indie bookseller associations help promote regional authors and regional books, so check out the association that covers the area where you live, the region in which your book takes place, or the region where you grew up and still have a lot of connections.

- Look at the author programs the associations offer and participate in those that will benefit you and/or your book.

- Consider the different advertising promotions they offer, from a banner on their website, a listing in their newsletter, or sponsorships at their yearly events.

- Use any assistance they give for connection with the book-sellers in that region.

- Consider attending their annual trade show.

- If speaking is your forte, look for speaking opportunities at the annual trade show or other events.

CHAPTER 18

AWARD ENTRIES

Winning awards for your book can help garner publicity and build your author brand. There are a variety of award programs available. Do your research and reach out to your publisher to see if they enter award programs for you, or if it is something you are expected to do for yourself.

If your publisher expects you to enter the award programs, they may have a list of programs they recommend. If you are self-published, you will need to enter on your own. Some award programs do not accept self-published books, and other programs are specifically designed for self-published books.

There are many award programs available:

- Indie Awards
- IPPY Awards (Independent Publisher Book Awards)
- American Library Association Awards
- National Book Awards
- Awards sponsored by specific organizations such as IBPA
- Regional bookseller association awards

Most award programs are for front-list books (books that have been published within a year), so it is important to stay on top of submitting award applications as soon as your book is eligible. Some award programs have fees for submission while others are free. Some award programs have cash prizes, and others have seals and publicity as the prize.

Award programs should be a part of your marketing plan. Search online for "book award programs" to identify programs that are appropriate for your book. Then get the submission into your marketing calendar and follow their instructions to the letter.

CHAPTER 19

ONGOING MARKETING

S ome authors seem to believe that marketing is important only around the release of a book because that is where publishers and distributors put their attention, but that assumption is not correct. With any business and any product, ongoing marketing is a necessity to keep the product in the eye of the target market. Where a book is concerned, that means keeping it accessible to readers and continuing to expand your fan base and your level of discoverability.

Once your book is in the marketplace, the marketing side of things changes a bit. If you have a publisher and distributor, your book slips from a front-list title to a backlist title after the year it releases, and sales reps are no long bringing it to the attention of retailers. At that point, it is up to you to continue to create buzz about your book.

Book Reviews

It is important to understand that ongoing reader reviews continue to be important for the entire life of a book, so securing reviews and soliciting reader reviews should be a part of your marketing plan every year.

- In your newsletter, blog, or on social media, remind readers about the importance of reviews and how they can continue to help your success.

- Your book will benefit from reviews no matter how long your book has been in the marketplace, even if it's years after it has been released.

- The more reviews a book has on Amazon, Goodreads, Book-Bub, Barnes & Noble, etc., the more intriguing it is for potential readers. Potential new readers are always available, even for bestselling books that have sold millions of copies.

For more information on book reviews and endorsements, please refer to chapter 8, "Book Reviews and Endorsements." For more information about Amazon reviews, please refer back to chapter 9, "The Power of Amazon." You can also refer to chapter 11, "BookBub," for further information.

Using a Newsletter for Ongoing Marketing

As we have previously discussed, creating and sending an author newsletter can be one of the most powerful marketing tools an author has. And this is true, not only as you launch your book, but even years after your title has been released.

Continuing to have a newsletter should be a go-to marketing tool for an author. You're a writer, so writing a newsletter should easily fall into your skill set. A newsletter is not just "all about your book"; it is a tool to help you to connect with your followers, build new followers, and help your fans get to know you better. As the years roll by, you may change the frequency of your newsletter, depending on whether you have written other books or how busy your author appearance schedule is, but maintaining a newsletter is important.

Please refer to chapter 3 about how to create a newsletter.

Reusing Your Content

When you write a book, you create content. When you place it in the marketplace, you are marketing. One of the cornerstones of marketing is to reuse your content in as many creative ways as possible.

- Have your book in as many formats as possible. Your publisher will most likely publish your book in these popular formats:
  - Print
  - eBook
  - Audiobook
- Blog
  - Reuse the content or premise of your book in a blog. For instance, if you've written a nonfiction book about grieving, your blog can cover a wide variety of subjects around grieving.
  - If you've written genre fiction, i.e. a mystery, your blog can have segments about writing a mystery, developing your characters, or some of the mysteries you've read that got you interested in writing mysteries.
- Social media
  - Use your social media platforms for cover reveals, quotes about your book, small blurbs from your book, etc.
- Website
  - Reuse your content by having a cover reveal or sharing excerpts from your book available to entice new readers, etc.

Keeping Your Title Active after the Year of Release

In the publishing world, both publishers and authors usually concentrate marketing attention on books before they release, or the first six to nine months after they release. But there is no expiration date on a book, so it can be viable for a very long time. *How to Win Friends and Influence People* by Dale Carnegie is a good example. That book was published in the early 1900s and is still often used or referred to today.

The next sections discuss some of the tools you can use to keep your book in the spotlight or bring it back into the spotlight.

Giveaways

Authors often use book giveaway promotions to expand their discoverability to a wider range of readers and to get the book (print and/or eBook) plus book marketing collateral into the hands of readers, which can help in word-of-mouth marketing.

Readers like giveaways because they open opportunities for them to win promotional items:

- Free books
- Bookmarks
- Pens
- Posters
- Mugs

There are a variety of websites that offer opportunities for conducting a book giveaway. Most of the sites will charge for the giveaway, so the author will have the expense of both creating the giveaway on the site and the prizes.

Below is a list of sites that offer giveaway promotions. You will want to check out each site individually to find out the rules and guidelines of their particular giveaway options.

- Amazon
- Goodreads
- Rafflecopter

- Social media sites
  - Facebook
  - Instagram
  - Twitter
  - YouTube

Do a search on the internet for other sites that offer book giveaway opportunities. You can also offer free books through your website the way *New York Times* bestselling author James Patterson does.

Donate

Consider donating your book to:

- Hospitals
- Shelters
- Churches
- Libraries
- Doctor/dental offices
- Organizations or clubs, which can help readers discover your book

Price Campaigns

Price campaigns—where the price on your print book, eBook, or audiobook is temporarily reduced to entice buyers—can be used to bring focus to your book no matter how long it has been in the marketplace. These campaigns are typically done with eBooks or audiobooks since you do not have the expense of inventory with these formats.

If you have self-published, you can create these campaigns yourself. If you have a publisher, you will need to work with them to create a price campaign. Most publishers continuously work with their distributors to create price campaigns, especially for eBooks and audiobooks.

- Price campaigns are most effective with eBooks because costs on print books can tip upside down very quickly.

- You will need a communication vehicle to market a price campaign. Just lowering the price on your eBook is not going to be very effective. Let the reading public know that your book is on sale and why they should buy it. Typically, social media posts alone are not enough unless you have thousands of followers, but they can help promote a sale.

- BookBub is a great way to promote a price campaign. Please refer to chapter 11.

- When a price campaign is active, follow your title on Amazon. When you notice that your book has hit number one in a category on Amazon, or in the top ten in a category, etc., make sure you promote it on social media with a screenshot.

Active Social Media Presence

Continue your social media presence and campaign long after the release date of your book.

- Pinterest and Instagram are both very visual and use images as a means of communication, so create "visual stories of you, your brand, and your work" to entice existing fans and new readers.

- Use social media to encourage your fans to market your book.

- Participate in a podcast tour. The internet is a great source for finding existing podcast tours.

- Increase your visibility with guest blogging for bloggers who have a strong following.

Free Publicity Opportunities

Opportunities for free publicity are readily available if you keep your eyes open for them, both in your local community and in online communities as well. Below are just a few ideas to get you thinking and watching.

HARO

Sign up for Help a Reporter Out (HARO), a sourcing service that connects writers with relevant experts (https://www. helpareporter.com/sources).

- You'll get an email two to three times per day that includes media opportunities.
- Find opportunities that match with your experience and/or your book and respond to the email address given.
- You may have a chance to be quoted in articles, which can help garner publicity.

Appear on podcasts

- As an "expert" on the writing process, the creative life, selling books, coming up with ideas for books, etc.

Be aware of what's happening in your community

- Article or column opportunities in local papers or magazines
- Local events that need speakers

Capitalize on Current Events

If you can strategically promote a book during specific seasons, an annual event, or when something pops up in the media, take advantage of the opportunity. For example:

- If you're a romance writer, do a marketing push close to Valentine's Day.

- If appropriate, promote your book as a summer beach read or as an airplane read during the holidays.

- If your book features athletes overcoming great obstacles, promote it during the MLB or NFL playoffs or a relevant spring event.

- Strategically take advantage of what's trending in the news if it's relevant to your book.

Here are some marketing tools you can use during strategic times:

- Social media pushes
- Price campaign
- Advertising campaign
- Write articles that tie your book topic or genre to current interests
- Facebook Live events

CHAPTER 20

KEEPING YOUR BOOTS ON THE GROUND

Long-term success is dependent on you as an author continuing to "get out there" for people to learn about you and your book. Authors who put "boots on the ground" help their publishers, distributors, and bookstores in selling their books. The stronger brand an author has, the stronger sales pitch you can make to promote and sell your books. Stay active and keep being present in the world of books and readers. Have confidence in yourself, your book(s), and your creativity.

How to Stay Active

- Continue to gain exposure at local events (art fairs, library, bookstores, schools, etc.).

- Book clubs and/or reading groups review both front list and backlist books, so continue to seek them out.

- Seek out appearances at book festivals and participate in events, including being on panels, that you are invited to.

- Attend and/or exhibit at larger events where people who love books and reading congregate.

- Look for writers' groups where you can speak or attend. Helping new writers can help build your brand and fan base.

- Attend writers' conferences (writers are readers too).

- Seek out speaking opportunities.

- Depending on the topic of your book, you may want to organize workshops.

- Make your vacations work for you. If you're heading to a new locale for vacation, do some advanced research and set up readings and/or visits at their local libraries, schools, bookstores, etc.

Publish New Books

Nothing sells backlist like front list. Publishing new books can help you garner a wider audience. If a reader likes a book you've written, they'll want to check out other books you've written.

Another suggestion would be to write a series. There are many additional marketing opportunities available for a book series than for a standalone book.

So keep writing and submitting those books for publishing.

GET READY, GET SET, SUCCEED!

There is something magical about writing and publishing a book as your ideas and concepts go from your imagination onto the paper and then into a book that you can hold in your hands. That process takes a lot of steps and energy, but the final product is well worth it.

Marketing your book can be just as magical if you put the same type of imagination, energy, and passion into it. Your marketing plan can be the roadmap for putting your book into the hands of people who will be entertained, informed, and changed by your story or ideas.

Our goal in writing this book was to provide a roadmap for you to create a successful book marketing plan. As you now know, marketing is an involved process, but it doesn't need to be overwhelming. Put your own personal stamp on how you want to approach marketing your book. Stay organized and stay the course.

Our best advice to authors when it comes to marketing a book is the same advice we give to writers, and that is to enjoy the process! Remember, marketing is a marathon, not a sprint.

Happy marketing!

ABOUT THE AUTHORS

erri Ann Leidich has been at the helm of Boutique of Quality Books Publishing Company for over a decade and has grown it from a startup with two books to a mid-sized independent publisher with two imprints (BQB Publishing and WriteLife Publishing). Her publishing company has received national recognition, and has a full catalog of many award-winning titles. Each day, she deals with book marketing—both from a publisher's perspective and from the perspective of how crucial an author's participation in marketing is. She understands that while books need to be high quality before entering the marketplace, it is the marketing that will help both the book and author succeed.

Terri is also a writer (when she has time) and a published author. She lives in the mountains of North Carolina with her husband Glenn.

J **ulie Bromley** has many years of experience working alongside authors providing marketing and personal assistant services. She puts quality of service along with integrity and client confidentiality above all else. Happy to be behind the scenes, Julie owns Signed Books and Stuff, a boutique UK marketing and distribution service along with support services to authors all around the globe. She is also the marketing manager for BQB Publishing and WriteLife Publishing where she guides and directs marketing efforts.

On a personal note, Julie lives in England, UK, with her husband, their children, and a crazy Patterdale Terrier called Loki. Her hobbies include reading, traveling, charity work, and game night with the family.

OTHER BOOKS BY TERRI ANN LEIDICH

W hen Terri Ann Leidich's twenty-year-old son was sud-
denly killed in a vehicle accident, she was thrown into the
roller coaster agony of grief. Adapted from the journal
she kept through the experience of her horrendous loss, this book
is a roadmap for parents who have lost children, as well as for
those who are on the sidelines watching the agony of someone
they care about and not knowing what to do or how to help.

Terri Ann's ability to put emotions and experiences into words
that everyone can understand and relate to can shine as a beacon
of hope and understanding during a time of excruciating pain.

When someone is grieving over the loss of a loved one, it is often hard to know how to be there for them, even though we want to. With the poetry and verse she wrote during her own journey through the grief of losing her son, along with beautiful photography that supports the emotion of her words, Terri Ann Leidich gives a voice to those who are grieving and healing.

Designed to be a gift to someone in grief, this book puts words to emotions, gives feelings to the confusion, and lends hope at a time that can feel hopeless. Whether it is a gift to yourself or a gift to someone you care about who is suffering the pain of loss, this book will offer understanding, hope, support, and love.

alled to the bedside of their dying mother, the Miller sisters—Helene, Suzanne, and Alice—reluctantly return to their childhood home in northern Minnesota. What should be a reunion of love and warmth is tainted by the ghosts of their childhood. Their parents' farm is a place of painful memories. With their mother slipping into a coma, the sisters are left with the troubles of their current lives and the bitterness of their childhood. But as they begin to reconnect, bond, and see themselves through each other's eyes, together they tread through the wreckage of the past to create lives filled with hope, love, and triumph.